Heinrich Preschers

Letters to the directors and Proprietors of East-India Stock

and to Edmund Burke

Heinrich Preschers

Letters to the directors and Proprietors of East-India Stock and to Edmund Burke

ISBN/EAN: 9783744715683

Printed in Europe, USA, Canada, Australia, Japan

Cover: Foto ©Suzi / pixelio.de

More available books at **www.hansebooks.com**

TO THE DIRECTORS AND PROPRIETORS OF EAST-INDIA STOCK; AND TO THE RIGHT HONOURABLE EDMUND BURKE.

LONDON:
Printed for J. FIELDING, No. 23, Pater-noster Row.
M.DCC.LXXXII.

To the Directors and the Proprietors of East-India Stock.

Gentlemen,

I EARNESTLY recommend the following letters to your candid and diſpaſſionate peruſal. They are written with no view to party. The queſtion ſoon to be determined is, Whether you ſhall tacitly eſtabliſh a precedent of the moſt dangerous tendency, or reſiſt it effectually in the firſt inſtance. A right honourable Member of the Houſe of Commons, from whom I ſhould have expected more attention to the rights of Engliſhmen, has told us, that the Court of Proprietors have nothing to do in the removal of Mr. Haſtings. Before we conſider the very extraordinary merits of our Governor-General, before we know any thing of the man intended to ſucceed him; let us determine how far a Vote of the Houſe of Commons is to bind us.—Every lawyer in the kingdom, every honeſt man, will tell us, that a Vote of the Houſe of Commons is not binding upon any chartered Company in this

this kingdom, or indeed upon any individual, their own members excepted. If the Legiſlature ſhould think proper to deprive us of the ſervices of Mr. Haſtings, we muſt of courſe ſubmit; but let us not remove ſuch a man ourſelves without the cleareſt conviction of the wiſdom and expediency of the meaſure. — The Swallow packet is fortunately arrived: ſhe will bring in a complete relation of the affair of Benares: ſhe will bring down the tranſactions in Bengal to the commencement of the preſent year. Let the diſpatches be coolly and conſiderately read: let Mr. Haſtings's merits be impartially conſidered — let the character of his intended ſucceſſor be fairly canvaſſed; and then let us come to a determination upon a point, in which not only our future welfare, but our very exiſtence will depend.

I am,

GENTLEMEN,

Your moſt obedient humble ſervant,

An Independent Proprietor.

June 3d, 1782.

LETTERS

LETTERS

TO THE

PROPRIETORS of EAST-INDIA STOCK.

LETTER I.

THE present critical and interesting situation of your affairs, renders it particularly incumbent on every Proprietor of India-stock to attend to the proceedings of Parliament on this important occasion. On the resolutions they are about to take, the prosperity of your affairs abroad, and your existence as a Company, materially depend. In your capacity of English subjects, you have a right to watch the conduct of Parliament, and in that of Proprietors it is your interest to be peculiarly attentive to it. Whilst this right is exercised, and this interest asserted with decency and respect, I have not a doubt of your representations being listened to with attention. The sentiments of some of his Majesty's present ministers, regarding the Company, have been warm in support of their chartered rights, and liberal in professing a desire to free them from the shackles of government: with these assurances, we have every reason to hope they will not adopt any measures that are an invasion of the rights they profess to defend, or an infringement of the freedom they profess to encourage.

From the resolutions which have been proposed to Parliament by the Chairman of the Select Committee, and from opinions which have been very freely given, it is generally understood that Governor Hastings and the present Supreme Council will be removed. This removal may be effected, according to the act of 1774, by petition to the King from the Court of Directors, or by a new act of Parliament for the reasons to be assigned therein. In either case, the petition or the act will go to the establishing of some delinquency in the parties, or some insufficiency in the appointments. The resolutions of the Secret Committee speak plainly in terms of disapprobation of Mr. Hastings's political conduct; and they revert to matters so far back as the year 1772. What Mr. Hastings's conduct hath been, how much it was at first commended, what attempts were afterwards made to remove him, how they failed, and what honourable support the Proprietors gave him, it is not my present intention to enquire, neither shall I enter into a discussion of his merits, abilities, and experience. What I mean and wish is, to draw the attention of the Proprietors to a preservation of their own rights. When Parliament assert their power of removing the Supreme Council, for reasons which they in their wisdom declare to be insufficient, I listen with profound respect, but not with entire conviction; and since the wisdom, even of Parliament, is fallible, I may be permitted to doubt; but when I am told, they have a right to go a step farther, and appoint what persons they please to fill the stations of the Supreme Council, I hope I may be permitted to ask where is the freedom of the Company, where are its chartered rights, and above all, where is the emancipation from Government?

If Parliament can remove any set of men, and appoint any other, as often as they please, without consulting the Proprietors,

Proprietors, the power of the latter muſt be annihilated; and when they have loſt the power, I would adviſe them to relinquiſh the reſponſibility; but if the right of nominating their own ſervants be yet allowed them, I would then moſt earneſtly entreat them to be very circumſpect in the exerciſe of it. I entreat them to conſider the hazardous ſtep, in the firſt inſtance, of recalling, at this juncture, ſo old and able a ſervant as Mr. Haſtings; and in the ſecond, of ſending out a ſet of men who are ſtrangers to the country, its laws, its manners, its cuſtoms, language, and politics. Admitting that ſome parts of Mr. Haſtings's conduct may be exceptionable, are there not many which have received and deſerve applauſe? His abilities are confeſſed, even by his enemies, and his integrity they cannot accuſe. Will the Proprietors remove ſuch a man? And is there no medium between cenſure and diſmiſſion?

If Parliament were to paſs an act, as they ſeem to intend, for the guidance of the Company's government in India, I think one may venture to pronounce, from Mr. Haſtings's conduct, in the two firſt years of his government, that no man would adhere more ſtrictly to their orders. Whilſt he enjoyed the confidence of his maſters, they never found a more obedient or a more capable ſervant. When Government interfered, and introduced the unfortunate conteſts in the Supreme Council, which involved the Directors themſelves in party feuds, and when the inviſible agency of Miniſters ſerved to increaſe them, intemperate acts and heats were the conſequences both at home and abroad; and in this interval no permanent plan or ſyſtem was purſued: but ſince it is the benevolent intention of Parliament to guard againſt future error from paſt experience, and to preſcribe the mode of governing theſe diſtant provinces with the greateſt poſſible advantage to the ſtate, I would ſubmit it to their conſideration, and that of the Proprietors, whether theſe ends are likely to be anſwered by ſending utter ſtrangers into that country. If the Proprietors ſhould be of opinion, that there are no ſervants in that country, nor in this, who are worthy of a place in the Supreme Council, and if they think that no ſet of men can have reſided in India without being rendered unfit for ſuch a ſtation, or that the Legiſlature, with the power to appoint, hath alſo the power to endue others with knowledge, integrity, abilities, and experience, then let them join in the preſent meaſures, and try the fatal experiment of recalling Mr. Haſtings.

An INDEPENDENT PROPRIETOR.

April 18, 1782.

LETTER II.

IN a letter I addreſſed to you a few days ago, I gave my reaſons for calling your attention to the preſent ſituation of your affairs; and in the hope that my humble labours may not be unacceptable, I ſhall venture to dedicate them a little longer to your ſervice..

The ſubject which is now the object of enquiry and deliberation, hath, under different circumſtances, engaged the ſerious conſideration of the Proprietors and Parliament near twenty years. It is a ſubject, however, ſo difficult to be underſtood, it hath given riſe to ſo much controverſy, and it hath ſo excited the paſſions and prejudices of all orders of men, that it is not to be wondered at if many erroneous opinions have been entertained, and ſome falſe ſyſtems adopted. But ſince ſo much argument hath already been urged, and ſo much reaſoning hath already been employed, that the cleareſt underſtanding is puzzled, a few facts may, perhaps, impreſs the mind more forcibly than many arguments. If, alſo, experience is more ſure than theory, and that future effects may be judged of from ſimilar cauſes which have already occurred, a plain recital of ſome paſt occurrences, may, perhaps, lead us to a truer judgment of the ſubject, than any other mode of inveſtigation.

In the year 1763, your Government of Bengal was engaged in a war with Coſſim Ally Khan, and Sujah Dowlah, that threatened the exiſtence of the Company in as great a degree as the preſent war with Hyder Ally and the Mahrattas. The politics of the late Mr. Henry Vanſittart, were, at that period, as much deſcried as thoſe of Mr. Haſtings are now; and he, who hath ſince been acknowledged to have borne a moſt excellent character, was then traduced, aſperſed, and reviled with all the rage of party. In 1764, you judged it expedient, for the ſafety of the Company's poſſeſſions, and the reformation of the greateſt enormities (as they were then called,) to ſend out the late Lord Clive, at the head of a Select Committee, with ſpecial powers to reſtore peace, and correct abuſes. Upon their arrival in 1765, they found the enemy vanquiſhed, and peace reſtored; but the work of reformation they repreſented as one of the labours of Hercules, and compared the ſettlement of Calcutta to the Augæan ſtable. There was hardly a term of abuſe in the Engliſh language, which they did not apply to the ſervants of that time. At the beginning of 1767, his Lordſhip had finiſhed the great work of refor-

reformation, and eſtabliſhed the pacific ſyſtem ſo much applauded ſince.

In a very few years after his arrival in England, this truly great man and his colleagues were arraigned by Parliament: and ſuch was the violence of the proceedings, and the temper of thoſe times, that the very man who a few years before had received rewards and praiſes of the Company, honours from his King, and was ſtiled the "heaven born General," was on the point of being ſtripped of all his laurels, and was reviled as a plunderer and a murderer.— The language he had held to the Court of Directors againſt their ſervants, was retorted upon him, and he ſaw, and confeſſed the injuſtice he had done them. In the end he was acquitted; and we have ſeen men, in the very ſame Parliament, who then perſecuted him with rigour, and were earneſt for his condemnation, now eager to do juſtice to his memory, and retract their former opinions.

The pacific ſyſtem, which hath been lately celebrated as the only true one for the intereſt of the Company, and under which we have been ſaid to proſper, and be affluent, had not been eſtabliſhed above four years, when it was found to be ſo very defective, that an extraordinary and new commiſſion was granted to three Superviſors, with controuling powers over all the ſettlements. The unfortunate fate of the Aurora prevented our knowing the conſequence of this ſcheme.

In two years after this event, it appeared, the Company were upwards of two millions in debt, and obliged to throw themſelves into the hands of government, to prevent a bankruptcy. At this alarming period, Mr. Cartier, one of the beſt, and moſt amiable men in the world, was ſeverely cenſured for drawing bills on the Company, and he and ſome members of the Council were harſhly diſmiſſed.

Mr.

Mr. Haſtings was then looked up to as the only man who could retrieve your affairs; and for this purpoſe was ſent from your Preſidency of Madras to Bengal. He juſtified your choice; and by a moſt diligent exertion of his uncommon abilities, he found reſources to pay off your enormous debt of two millions and an half, and to reſtore you from bankruptcy to affluence. He received the warmeſt thanks of your Directors, and for two years they were laviſh in his praiſe.

In the year 1774 your affairs were again canvaſſed by Parliament, and an act paſſed, which put the government of Bengal, and all your ſettlements on an entire new footing. What the effects of this plan have been, I need not relate! Suffice it to ſay, that in the preſent year, 1782, you are again brought before the tribunal of Parliament; and if, as it is ſaid, the preſent government of Bengal, like all former adminiſtrations, are to be reviled and diſmiſſed, you may expect to have three, or five gentlemen ſent out, who may have a political exiſtence of as many years: and how long this circulation and change of men and meaſures may laſt, or rather, how ſoon it may put an end to your own exiſtence, is a problem that may, perhaps, be ſhortly reſolved.

I ſhall take another opportunity to remark upon the facts I have recited, and for the preſent I ſhall only obſerve, that they plainly ſhew the great difficulty of directing the affairs of a country ſo very remote, how very fluctuating and uncertain the opinions of men muſt be on ſuch diſtant tranſactions, and that the miniſterial plan of 1774 hath been the moſt pernicious of any which hath yet been tried.

An INDEPENDENT PROPRIETOR,

April 20, 1782.

LETTER III.

IN my laſt Letter I gave you a ſummary detail of your affairs, and the various plans which had been tried for the laſt twenty years: I therein ſhewed you, what different opinions had prevailed of the ſame men at different times, what a variety of means had been purſued for the ſame end, and how inadequate they had all proved: I then drew one general concluſion, which was, the difficulty of judging of the moſt proper meaſures to be adopted for the government of ſo remote a country; and I ſhall now take leave to be more particular in my inference, and endeavour to apply the paſt examples to the preſent occaſion.

I think the preſent ſituation of Bengal may be aptly compared to what it was in the year 1764, when the late Lord Clive and his Select Committee were ſent out to reſtore peace and correct abuſes. A dangerous and expenſive war was juſt concluded at that time, and the peace they went out to make, they found eſtabliſhed on their arrival. From the laſt advices by the way of Buſſorah we are informed, hoſtilities had virtually ceaſed between the Mahrattas and General Goddard; that Mhadajee Scinda had concluded a treaty, and was going with Mr. Anderſon to negotiate a general peace at Poonah; that the Nizam and Mhoodajee Bhooſlah had alſo become mediators; and that Sir Eyre Coote had obliged Hyder to retire from the Carnatic. If, to this account, we add the arrival of the reinforcement from Europe, I hope I ſhall not be thought too ſanguine, or to force the compariſon I mean to make, if I ſay, it is more than probable that the perſons, who are to

be

be sent into the Supreme Council at Bengal, will, as Lord Clive did, find it in perfect tranquillity. In this case, they will, like their predecessors, turn their thoughts to the more arduous task of reformation; and, like them, they will paint a gloomy picture of your distress. They will tell you, they found the country drained of all its wealth, its revenues ruined by the iron hand of rapacious collectors, the mode of collections defective in all its parts, the administration of justice totally corrupt, the servants of the Company sunk into luxury and dissipation, and that hydra, corruption, rearing his seven, or fifty heads, as they may be in the humour to paint him.

To restore a country from so deplorable a state as this requires no common talents, and you may again be told, as you have already been informed, with a very becoming modesty in the men who drew their own characters, "that a degree of virtue and ability, not to be found in common men, must be exerted in this arduous task." The next consideration is, where are men to be found of this description, and by whom are they to be chosen? Parliament will tell you, — not in your service; they are all too much tainted with the principles of their education there, and too much concerned in the abuses which are to be corrected, to be trusted with such power. No! Men of these rare virtues are to be found only in the incorrupt legislature of this kingdom; and, after they have been duly qualified, by being members of a Select or Secret Committee on India affairs for a session or two, they will then have put on the whole armour of knowledge and virtue, and will be completely equipped for the combat of reformation. They will tell you also, the wild schemes of conquest and ambition are as repugnant to your true interests as the corrupt plans of peculation; these, therefore, must be carefully provided against, and the illustrious characters of Rustam and Effendi must now be held up as objects of horror, not as examples of imitation; and, if there be any foundation for the rumour which is gone abroad, we shall have reason to acknowledge the paternal care of Parliament, in this respect at least, by the persons who are supposed to be the objects of its choice, except indeed, in the instance of the noble General, who has acquired a fame as immortal as those celebrated warriors by his indefatigable labours.

After these gentlemen have resided as long as is requisite for the great business of the public and themselves, and have rung the same changes upon abuses, reformation, corruption, and depravity, with their innumerable train of evils, and when they can with truth assure you, that, by their unremitted endeavours, the very reverse of this destructive system hath been established; they will return to their native land full of honours, though not of riches, in expectation of a peaceable enjoyment of the moderate income they have hardly earned by a painful industry. But behold the ingratitude and fickleness of a nation they have so honourably and faithfully served! They find committees of the House, both secret and select, sitting in judgement upon, and condemning that conduct which, in their own ideas, merited so much applause; and if Mr. Hastings doth not carry his notions of integrity too far, and will not scruple to obtain a seat in that House at the expence of a moral and political obligation, they may, perhaps, find him in one of the places they had left.

From the facts I have already stated of the former conduct of gentlemen upon precisely similar occasions, I do not think that this is an unnatural picture, or a forced conclusion. But let us turn from this to another object, perhaps more worthy of your consideration, namely, your right

right to make a choice of your own ſervants, and that emancipation which is to form a part of the general reformation, the preſent miniſters have ſo generouſly promiſed, and ſo honourably begun. If Parliament will both diſmiſs and appoint the ſervants who are to govern your affairs, and the Lords of the Treaſury are to regulate the orders of your Directors to thoſe ſervants, in what does your freedom conſiſt? If you are told that your intereſts are inſeparable from the nation's, and that it is their duty to watch over this valuable part of the empire in this manner. I have only to reply, that this argument proves the Company are not free in the ſenſe they ought to be. But if the preſent miniſters mean fairly, meet them fairly upon liberal grounds. Let there be no clandeſtine negotiations with Lords of the Treaſury and their Secretaries, but aſſert to the Legiſlature what you deem to be your rights. Bring it to this ſhort iſſue, that you think you ought to have the power of appointing and diſmiſſing your own ſervants, and that their proper line of duty to the nation, is, their own excellent idea of giving a general outline for the plan of government, and of controuling the conduct of the Court of Directors by Committees of Parliament. Let the Proprietors treat with Parliament upon enlarged ideas, and on terms worthy of men, who have one common good in view. On theſe principles let them aſk whether they are to have the actual appointment of their own ſervants, and the real conduct of their own affairs, without any other interference of Parliament than the general ſuper-intending controul of their Committees. If the anſwer be as candid as the queſtion is fair, you can have no doubt of what is then your duty. If the right be granted, a proper exerciſe of it is your firſt object; if it be denied, your next is, to reject the reſponſibility.

AN INDEPENDENT PROPRIETOR.

LETTER IV.

UPON the idea that Parliament mean not to restrict their enquiries merely to what they may think wrong in the conduct of Mr. Hastings, and from any past errors to prescribe such rules for a future Governor as they may think right, but that they will accompany their censure with dismission, and proceed even to new appointments, I have presumed to hint an opinion that such resolutions will affect your chartered rights. Pursuing the same idea, I will venture a little farther into the subject.

Some of the present ministers have been free to declare, that the act of 1774 infringed your ancient constitution, and all agree, that your affairs have not been better conducted since the interference of Parliament. I have already said, that Parliament act consistently with their professions, and take the true line of power and duty, when they inspect the conduct of your Directors, and regulate the political rules by which they would have your servants guided; but that, when they step beyond this line, and deprive you of the right of appointing your own servants, they break in upon the regularity of the system, and destroy the harmony of its parts. If Parliament should say that they do this, because you are not capable of conducting your own affairs, that you have no servants worthy of such a trust, and that therefore they make these appointments to preserve this valuable part of the empire to the nation; we should, in this instance, applaud their wisdom, as in all, we obey their power; but on a review of the past appointments, we cannot suppose these to have been their motives

motives. In 1774, they appointed two of your old servants; to these they added two general officers and a clerk in the War-office. In 1776, they gave you a linen-draper, and in 1781, you were furnished with a purser's clerk, and a director. Hath your interest been consulted in these appointments? Or hath your affairs been entrusted to better hands than you could have found in the line of your service? I think I may safely answer in the negative.

Amongst the exclusive rights and privileges of your charter, none, in my humble opinion, is more essential to the good government of your affairs than the appointment of your own servants. It is on a proper choice of them that your welfare materially depends; for on their conduct you must rely, and to them much must be trusted. The appointments in the Supreme Council ought to be looked up to by your servants, as the greatest reward, as dismission is certainly the greatest punishment; and since rewards and punishments are the two great hinges on which all governments turn, that system must be radically defective which is deprived of them. It is to the power, who confers the honour and can inflict the disgrace to which men naturally look in the first instance, consequently the intermediate body is considered only in an inferior or secondary degree; and whether this may not induce the Directors to think more lightly of their responsibility, and the servants less respectfully of the Directors authority, is a matter worthy your serious consideration. At all events it is an irregular and unnatural system that you should have an exclusive right to the management and trade of those countries, and that the first officers in them should be independent of your choice or censure. The pernicious effects of this system you are labouring under at this instant, and yet it is said, it is still to be continued.

If

If we are to believe an opinion which is very prevalent, and I confess my humble connections do not admit of my obtaining better authority than public report; the candidates for the station of Governor-General are General Smith and Mr. Francis. As you must in this case be deprived of Mr. Hastings's service for one of these gentlemen, it will be very proper for you to consider their different merits and qualifications, as they appear either on your records, or in those situations of life in which they have come under your observation, in order that you may judge wherein you are likely to be benefited by the change.

General Smith was originally an officer in your service on the coast of Coromandel, where he served with reputation, under those able Generals, Laurence, Clive, Coote, Monson, and Caillaud; he returned to England in 1762, with the rank of Major. Many of us recollect those circumstances, when party ran high in Leadenhall-street in 1763 and 1764, which induced the late Lord Clive to procure him the rank of Colonel in the King's service, and the post of second in command in Bengal. He arrived there in May, 1765. He commanded an army of observation in 1766. In 1767, he was promoted to the command of the army and third member of the Council and Select Committee; until the latter end of 1769, he resided chiefly out of your provinces at Allahabad. In the month of December, that year, he returned to England, and if report be true, with treble the fortune that Mr. Hastings *now* has, after more than thirty years service, and ten of these, Governor of Bengal.

Mr. Francis was forced upon you, and taken from a very humble line of life to be placed in the conspicuous station of a Supreme Counsellor; and from the peculiar circumstances of the times, and the bent of his talents, he was

more

more than a " ſilent ſenator." His pen was not of leſs uſe than his caſting voice to the gentlemen whoſe plans he defended by the former, and whoſe meaſures were carried by the latter. Endued with a quick apprehenſion, and abilities rather ſprightly than ſolid, aſſiſted by the knowledge of others in the revenues, and happy in his manner of dreſſing the materials with which he was furniſhed, he hath gained a reputation for knowledge more ſpecious than real.

Mr. Haſtings hath been bred from a very early period of life in your ſervice. To great abilities and a perfect knowledge of the language, laws, cuſtoms and manners of the people of India, is joined an experience of upwards of thirty years. He hath been tried in every rank and ſtation in your ſervice, and in all he hath given undoubted proofs of an unſhaken integrity. He reſtored your affairs from the loweſt ebb to their higheſt grandeur. He hath raiſed larger revenues, found more reſources, opened more channels of trade, and ſent home larger inveſtments than any of his predeceſſors. To his great exertion, and that deciſive conduct which marks the man of genius, are you greatly indebted for the ſafety of the Carnatic. The plan of relief, ſo ably executed by that camplete General, Sir Eyre Coote, was propoſed by Mr. Haſtings, and carried into effect by his caſting voice.

This is a very ſummary, perhaps imperfect ſketch of the public characters of theſe gentlemen, and I may not probably have done juſtice to the merits of any of them; indeed my only aim, in what I have ſaid, is to induce you to examine more thoroughly into the pretenſions of each, that if the deciſion be left to you, you may make it with propriety.

AN INDEPENDENT PROPRIETOR.

LET-

LETTER V.

THERE are ſome material points I have only hinted at in my former Letters, which, as they deſerve your moſt particular attention, may not be unworthy of a farther diſcuſſion. The firſt is, that you ſhould endeavour, by every poſſible means, to re-eſtabliſh yourſelves and your ſervice, upon that independent footing, to which your charters give you the faireſt claim. The next is, that you ſhould revert to your true conſtitutional plan, of promoting your own ſervants to thoſe honours, which ought to be the reward of faithful ſervices.

I have explained myſelf ſo freely, in regard to the controuling power of Parliament, and to what line that power ſhould limit itſelf, that I hope my meaning cannot be miſtaken in the expreſſion of—independent footing; but leſt any doubt ſhould remain, I will be ſtill more explicit, and ſay, that footing on which you conducted your affairs, before Parliament appointed a Supreme Council and a Supreme Court of Judicature, and before Miniſters made patronage in the eaſt a ſupplement to that of the weſt. If we may be allowed to judge from experience, your original plan was certainly the beſt; for ſince the interference of the one, and the influence of the other, your councils have been diſtracted abroad, your Directors divided at home, and your whole ſervice falling to decay.

In conſidering the next point of promoting your own ſervants, I am naturally led to the ſubject I touched upon in my laſt Letter, regarding a proper choice of perſons to fill the important ſtations in your Supreme Council; and conformably

formably to thoſe principles on which I ground my own opinion, and preſume to offer it to you, I would reject Mr. Francis's offers to return to Bengal, becauſe he was not bred in your ſervice. I hope both Parliament and ourſelves will have too much liberality to make invidious compariſons of talents or of principles; but giving Mr. Francis full credit for his ſhare of both, I am ſure he will not ſuffer in either, if I declare my opinion, that you have ſervants not at all inferior to him in theſe reſpects; and his having been once forced into your ſervice, can ſurely never be made a plea for the ſame injuſtice.

The removal of Mr. Haſtings, and particularly at this juncture, is another point at which I have hinted; but it is in my humble opinion, a ſubject of ſo much importance, and involves ſo many conſequences, that I do ſeriouſly hope, when Parliament conſider the ſervices *he hath performed*, the abilities *he hath diſplayed*, and the proofs *he hath given* of uncorrupt conduct and ſpotleſs integrity, they will not deprive the Company of the benefit of theſe abilities, and this integrity, for what they may deem errors in judgment, or becauſe his politics have proved rather unfortunate in the event than unwiſe in the plan.

But if political errors are to be alledged as reaſons for the removal of Mr. Haſtings, they ought, in fairneſs of argument, to be equally cogent againſt the appointment of any other perſon who may have fallen into them; and by the ſame parity of reaſoning, it may be aſked, whether General Smith adopted a wiſe policy, in keeping a brigade at Allahabad, and depriving the provinces, by its being paid out of them, of 300,000l. of circulating ſpecie annually? Whether it was a prudent meaſure to have adviſed a deputation in 1768, to the Vizier, which was expenſive and uſeleſs, and whether it was judicious to have propoſed a plan for opening the Company's Treasury, which reduced them to bankruptcy, and for only consenting to which, the virtuous Mr. Cartier was dismissed your service.

The peculiar hardship of Mr. Hastings's situation, calls for more than common candour from Parliament and the Proprietors. He is tried by the severest test which can be applied, and under such circumstances as hardly any conduct can escape from censure. Judgment hath been passed on the success of his measures, not on the wisdom of their design. Plans, which were ably formed, have been condemned, because they were weakly executed. He is arraigned at a tribunal, where he cannot plead his own cause, and to which his most inveterate enemy hath been admitted as a principal witness.

When the mind hath been long intent upon one subject, it is liable to be heated by its own reasonings, and a false glare will sometimes dazzle the clearest understanding; one train of ideas is often pursued with an eagerness that excludes any other, and our utmost caution will not always guard us against prejudice. To some such cause, or to some imperfection of our nature, must we attribnte an inference in the last Report of the Select Committee, that imputes to Mr. Hastings his being accessary to the prosecution of Nundcomar, at a time when he had brought an accusation against him. I will be bold to say, that if the gentlemen of the Committee will take the pains to sift that matter thoroughly, they will be convinced Mr. Hastings was not only ignorant of the apprehending of Nundcomar, but that his conduct would then, as it will now, stand the severest examination; and, as a proof that Mr. Hastings had nothing to fear from that accusation, which it is insinuated he shrunk from, *the very same charge* was afterwards renewed to *the very same Council*, and a particular committee appointed by

them,

them, consisting of Messrs. Maxwell, Anderson, and Grant, to examine into this affair. Their commission lasted some months, and, after the most minute investigation, it appeared, there was not the least foundation for the charge. This is a matter of fact, capable of instant proof, for the Diary of their proceedings is, or ought to be, amongst the records of the India House. It is much to be lamented, that, where facts were to be established, insinuations should have been resorted to, and the gentlemen would have done well to consider, that if any of them should apply to fill those stations their reports tend to vacate, how forcibly the argument of inference may be retorted upon them.

I have been led to make this remark on a paragraph of the Report of the Select Committee, because, when I am contending for the character of Mr. Hastings, and recommending him to your protection, I am unwilling that an impression should remain on your minds to his prejudice, which it is in my power to remove; and I am confident, from the characters of the gentlemen of the Committee, that they will be equally glad with yourselves to have any point cleared up, which may affect the character of an individual, whose conduct may be the object of their enquiry.

An INDEPENDENT PROPRIETOR.

LETTER VI.

IN the letters I have hitherto troubled you with, I have endeavoured to draw your attention to the preservation of your own rights, and to induce you to turn your thoughts to the appointment of a proper perſon to be your Governor General. If I ſhould have been fortunate enough to have ſuggeſted any hint that may be uſeful, or ſtarted any idea that may be improved by your better judgment, I ſhall have anſwered every purpoſe that the principles on which I have written, prompted me to hope for. But the temper of the preſent times, is, perhaps, too violent for an appeal to calm reaſon. I ſee, and dread the powerful effects of eloquence urged to its utmoſt exertions, by a heated imagination. The paſſions are again rouſed, and the ſtream of prejudice, which had either ſlackened or been diverted into other channels, now returns with redoubled force. Your ſervants in India can do nothing right. Their wars are plans of thunder; their treaties are compacts of injuſtice; and theirſelves monſters of iniquity. Theſe are the topics on which declamation delights to indulge; a thouſand cauſes contribute to their being liſtened to with applauſe; and if one inſtance be found to juſtify a particular ſtigma, the principle becomes general, and the concluſion is applied to all. To ſuch lengths hath this indiſcriminating ſpirit proceeded, that political conduct hath been tried by the teſt of moral rectitude, and claims, which originated in conqueſt, are to be reconciled to equity. If ſyſtems like theſe were adopted by the ſpeculative moraliſt, and ſupported by ingenious reaſoning, the novelty would not be much to be wondered at; and the arguments might ſerve to amuſe, though they did not convince: But when theſe ſentiments are carried into practical life, I fear the world is not refined enough to adopt them; and however right we might be in our principles, it is much to be apprehended the conſequences would be fatal. Let us only ſuppoſe the moral plan to be put into execution, and orders to be given that as it was the greateſt degree of injuſtice to with-hold the

Mogul's

Mogul's tribute, the arrears ſhall be paid him to the preſent time; that, as it was equally wrong to deprive him of the provinces of Corah and Allahabad, they ſhall be immediately made over to the Mahratta Chief, to whom his Majeſty granted a phirmaun for their poſſeſſion; that the arrears of Chout, which have been unjuſtly with-held from the Mahrattas, be paid as ſoon as poſſible the ſtate of the treaſury will admit, and that in the mean time, the proviſion of goods for Europe be prohibited, in order to afford a larger proportion of the revenues to liquidate this juſt claim.

There are ſeveral other demands, which, according to this moral reformation, would require a ſimilar adjuſtment; but theſe inſtances may, perhaps, be ſufficient to evince that, as moral virtue neither is, nor can be always practiſed in affairs of government, ſo it is unreaſonable to make it the ſtandard for political tranſactions. Without ſuffering ourſelves to be deceived by the ſpeculative arguments of ingenious men, and without miſleading ourſelves by a vain expectation of more virtue than is practiſed in human affairs, let us endeavour to ſeek that good which is attainable, and to eſtabliſh that rectitude which is practicable. Let ſome conſiſtent plan be formed, applicable to the manners, cuſtoms, and religion of the people, for whom it is intended; commit the execution of that plan to your ſervants, and puniſh them if they diſobey it. But if you are neither to form your own plans, nor have the controul of your own ſervants; if laws are to be forced upon you, that annihilate the powers of your government, and alienate the minds of the people you are to govern; if a ſyſtem, compoſed of jarring elements, is intruded upon you, how is it poſſible your ſervants ſhould act without offending the law or betraying your intereſt? A more diſtreſsful dilemma cannot be be conceived, and we have a ſtriking proof, that a laudable endeavour to compoſe the inevitable ſtrife of oppoſite contentions, is likely to be puniſhed as a criminal action.

With all theſe proofs of hypothetical reaſoning, let us not recur to it again. Let us endeavour to avail ourſelves of the aid of common ſenſe and the benefit of experience. Let us try whether the abilities which *have* proved uſeful to us in time of need, may not be ſo *again*. Let us appeal to facts, and not to theory. Whether the Mahratta war was juſtifiable or not, and whether the Court of Directors, or the Council of Bombay were right in their politics, is now a matter of ſpeculation; and the fact I would appeal to is, whether in the preſent ſituation, you can find a man ſo capable of ſupporting your drooping intereſts as Mr. Haſtings? I believe it is a fact, which will not be diſputed, that he hath found more reſources to aſſiſt your armies than any other man, and that he is now looked up to by the Preſidency of Madras and Sir Eyre Coote, as the moſt capable perſon of preſerving your power in India. It will be very difficult to tranfuſe the ideas of a Britiſh Houſe of Commons into the natives of Aſia; and an act, that ſeems wiſe to the enlightened underſtanding of the former, may have a contrary effect on the contracted minds of the latter; hence, however proper the legiſlature may think it to remove Mr. Haſtings, be aſſured the conſequence will be the very reverſe of what they intend; for in whatever light his conduct may be ſeen here, it is very certain the Indian powers behold it with admiration and reſpect; and however ludicrous the names of Ruſtum and Effendi, may ſound in England, moſt aſſuredly the compariſon does not convey a ridiculous idea to a native of Indoſtan.

Ambition and conqueſt, rapacity and injuſtice, are inexhauſtible themes for oratorial powers; and, in the preſent

diſpoſition

diſpoſition of men's minds, ſuch charges are admitted on the bare authority of an eloquent ſpeaker; but we, who ought to look to conſequences, and carefully to examine the truth of premiſes, ſhould not be ſeduced by the charms of eloquence, or biaſſed by the influence of prejudice. Our ſureſt guide is experience, and whilſt we have facts to appeal to, let us not have recourſe to ſuppoſition. Is your preſent Governor-General a rapacious man? his moderate fortune acquits him of ſuch an imputation. Hath any corrupt motive ever been attributed to him, which hath not been fully confuted when it was fairly brought forward? Witneſs the accuſation of Nundcomar, of which I ſpoke in my laſt letter. Have not his abilities been proved to you in various inſtances, and hath not he, on ſome important occaſions, reſcued you from diſtreſs? Witneſs the affluence he reſtored you to, when he firſt became your Governor, and his late exertions on the invaſion of the Carnatic. Is there a potentate in India who doth not reverence Mr. Haſtings? And did not the *Nizam* profeſs an implicit confidence in him, at a time that he had none in any of your other Preſidencies? In ſhort, there are ſo many proofs of Mr. Haſtings being poſſeſſed of ſuch rare virtues, and ſuch extraordinary abilities, and of his being ſo univerſally reſpected by all the powers in India, that the conſequence of recalling him, at this time, may be fatal to your affairs.

An INDEPENDENT PROPRIETOR.

LETTER VII.

I Can eaſily conceive that Mr. Haſtings's late miraculous eſcape from aſſaſſination ſhould be an unpardonable crime in the eyes of his thwarted competitors; but wherein he ſhould

ſhould be liable to cenſure for *his* part in thoſe reſolutions of the Supreme Council, which are ſuppoſed to have provoked the diabolical attack, is, I muſt own, far beyond the ſtretch of my ſagacity.

The motives which led this deed of horror, as far at leaſt as conjecture can trace them, are undiſputed to have ariſen from a demand made by the Governor General and Supreme Council, on Raja Cheyt Sing, a dependant and tributary Zemindar, for a trifling addition to his annual rent, in ſupport of three battalions of ſeapoys, during the continuance of the war with France. The ſeveral opinions and unanimous votes of the Supreme Council on this ſubject may be found in the Appendix to the Sixth Report of the Committee of Secrecy; and to thoſe authentic documents I refer, in proof of ſo much of the following conciſe narrative as relates to the right, the cauſe, and the extent of the demand in queſtion. The publication of that Appendix will, I hope, ſilence thoſe malicious miſrepreſentations which have hitherto deſignedly miſled the public.

The diſtricts of Gazypore and Benares are a portion of the Subah of Illahabad, and border on our province of Bahar. They produce an annual revenue of more than ſeventy lacks of rupees, from very low rents, and paid a tribute of twenty-four lacks yearly to the late Nabob, Vizier of Oud, Sujahud Doula; and it alſo appears from the evidence given by Captain Harper to the Select Committee, that they furniſhed a body of troops whenever the Vizier took the field, according to the eſtabliſhed conſtitution of the Mogul empire. The ſovereignty of thoſe diſtricts, with all its rights and revenues, was ceded to our Company in 1775, by the preſent Nabob Vizier, Aſof-ud-Doula. A ſunnud and cabooliet were executed in the uſual form, between the Supreme Council and Raja Cheyt Sing,

Sing, the Zemindar, by which he was bound to pay the ſame tribute he had hitherto furniſhed to the Nabob Vizier.

As from that moment the diſtricts of Gazypore, &c. became united and incorporated with the reſt of the Britiſh dominions in that part of India, the Governor-General produced in Council a propoſition for reducing Cheyt Sing's irregular, undiſciplined and unneceſſary troops, by adding a certain portion of them to our own army, to be paid, however, by him. It has always been a point of policy with the Company to diſcourage, and to prohibit, if poſſible, the maintenance of independent forces by any of the Indian powers under our protection. The Nabob of Bengal has none; the Nabob of Arcot has been frequently intreated, and at laſt with effect, to diminiſh his military eſtabliſhment; and the connivance to uſeleſs and dangerous bodies of troops, kept up by the Rajahs of ſome of the northern circars, forms a ſtrong article amongſt the objections made by the Court of Directors to the late Governor and Council of Madras. No political neceſſity, no ſtipulated exception, entitled Rajah Cheyt Sing to the peculiar privilege of a ſeparate army; nor was there any doubt of our right as well as power; as ſovereigns, to enforce the meaſure recommended by the Governor General, and it was over-ruled by the majority, merely on the plea of a compliment to the Rajah's deſires.

In 1778, in conſequence of the French war, our military eſtabliſhment in Bengal being greatly increaſed, it was propoſed in Council (and unanimouſly carried) to call on Cheyt Sing for ſome additional aid towards the ſupport of the very extraordinary expences of the ſtate; and it was expreſſly ſignified to him, that it was to continue during the war only. This, in fact, was nothing more than a modification of the Governor-General's original propoſition on our firſt acceſſion to the ſovereignty of Cheyt Sing's provinces, and which in time of profound peace it had not been thought neceſſary to enforce. The required addition was now very ſmall; five lacks of rupees, and was appropriated to the payment of three battalions of ſeapoys, with European officers. The propriety and juſtice, as well as neceſſity of this meaſure, immediately ſecured it the ſanction of the Court of Directors.

Hindoos are known to have a natural propenſity to hoarding, and Cheyt Sing poſſeſſes ample means for the gratification of this darling paſſion. It is notorious that he has ſaved at leaſt thirty lacks every year ſince he ſucceeded to the Zemindary, and including his father's treaſure, is ſuppoſed to keep locked up from circulation upwards of four millions ſterling in ſpecie.

Benares is now the richeſt city in India; a holy aſylum, ſanctified by the ſtrongeſt religious prejudices, and a crouded ſeminary of Indian literature. An almoſt imperceptible tax on its inhabitants, or the moſt trivial increaſe in the very low rents of the province, would have doubled our new demand: a proportionate reduction of the Rajah's uſeleſs troops would have anſwered the end, without any innovation whatever. Yet this avaricious wretch had the aſſurance to plead abſolute inability, and to pretend a neceſſity of ſelling his very furniture to pay the firſt year's quota; that of the ſecond year he roſolutely withheld, till extorted by threats of inſtant compulſion. Pretexts of poverty are ſeldom attended to by Indian governments, unleſs on manifeſt grounds: as theſe are become the ordinary and univerſal preliminaries to every payment from every debtor; and hence it is that no revenues are ever realized without the aſſiſtance of an armed force. But thoſe pretexts were peculiarly ſcandalous in the mouth of the richeſt inhabitant of Hindoſtan. The war has now continued four years,

and

and Cheyt Sing has probably paid twenty lacks of rupees on the whole (exclusive of his tribute) that is to say, two thirds of the savings of one year's rent; while the whole revenues of Bengal have been unavoidably mortgaged for the same state-necessity.

If this transaction be not within the line of reason, of justice, and of right: if any criminality whatever can be ascribed to the first proposers of it, there is no possible system of politics, no one act of any government, that can escape the ordeal. If neither the unanimity of a Council, which was hardly ever unanimous on any other point; if the full approbation of the Court of Directors, whose immediate province it was to decide; if the certainty of an inherent right existing in the Mogul Government, and proof positive from Captain Harper, of the actual exercise of that right; if the solemn cession of the sovereignty, with all its appendages, and the strong urgency of political necessity, will *not* altogether authorize the Company and the Company's servants to enforce so inconsiderable a demand on one of their acknowledged subjects, what will?

Good God! shall the commonest of all the common acts of government, the necessary provision of ways and means be termed a *robbery*? Shall the ruling power over twelve millions of people be arraigned in public, or calumniated in private, for impartially sharing among the several members of the state, that burthen which must unavoidably be borne some how by the whole? These are canons of justice, under which an angel could not be safe. But it should seem, that this new doctrine of robbery has already reached Benares; and that Cheyt Sing has, in consequence, conceived he might resist, or destroy the Governor-General of Bengal, with as little ceremony as he would a highwayman or a mad dog. Pardon the expression, I meant not to be jocular. The ſubject is much too ſerious and too alarming. Such a deliberate conſpiracy for aſſaſſinating a Governor and all his ſuite, while paſſing on affairs of political importance, through provinces immediately ſubjected to his authority! and that for ſo trifling a conſideration as fifty thouſand pounds to a man worth near five millions? It is impoſſible. Human nature revolts at the idea.

There muſt have been ſome concealed purpoſes of iniquity to be ſerved; ſome pernicious damned ſuggeſtions muſt have poiſoned his mind, and urged him to this temporary frenzy. Some deep complotting *Iago* has, by exaggerated powers of lies, laid the foundation for this deſperate act, and hood-winked the miſerable perpetrator, or he never could have been ſo blind to his own intereſt, to the little chance of ſucceſs, and the impoſſible of impunity. He never could otherwiſe have forgotten the conſequences of the unhappy maſſacre in his very neighbourhood at Patna.

He has probably, by this time, ſeen his folly as well as his guilt: I wiſh he may have found his tongue.

In the mean while, I muſt intreat the favour of thoſe gentlemen, who can ſtile the temporary and neceſſary increaſe of Cheyt Sing's tribute a *robbery*, to furniſh me with a term for this horrid attempt. I cannot trace even in idea, its enormous advance of criminality. I ſhould be glad too, that they would ſuggeſt a proportionate puniſhment, for I know not to what criminal juriſdiction Cheyt Sing may be amenable. I can only gueſs what proceſs his late Sovereign Shujah-ud-Doula would have followed on the occaſion; and, I fear, that may ſeem too ſevere to many Britiſh inquiſitors.

AN INDEPENDENT PROPRIETOR.

LET-

LETTER VIII.

It ſcarcely ever happens that, in any ſubject of controverſy, the original argument is ſtrictly adhered to. Plain queſtions of right and wrong are often puzzled by ſubtlety and ſophiſtry, till the mind knows not on which to decide. Art, prompted by intereſt, frequently conceals a ſimple truth, which common ſenſe and common honeſty would eaſily diſcover; and, in almoſt every debate, ſome artifice is practiſed by the contending parties. On ſubjects which affect the paſſions and intereſts of mankind, it is hardly poſſible to guard the mind from error and prejudice, or to prevent theſe diſingenuous methods of diſpute. Perhaps no ſubject was ever agitated in which the paſſions, prejudices, and intereſts of men were more excited, or concerned, than that of your government, and the conduct of your ſervants in India. It was not, therefore, to be expected that a committee of the Houſe of Commons ſhould be compoſed of men of ſuch equal tempers, as to be exempted from the common failings of their nature, or that ſome of theſe effects ſhould not be felt, in the courſe of a long enquiry.

From ſome late proceedings of the Select Committee, it appears, the great original deſign of their inſtitution hath been departed from, and that their enquiry hath become more perſonal than was intended by the Houſe, or even by themſelves; and it is much to be apprehended, that if they recede from general principles to particular inſtances, they may at laſt deſcend to party ſpirit, and perſonal conſiderations. To warn them of the danger of partiality might, perhaps, be deemed preſumption; but it is certainly my duty to guard you against the consequences of prepossession.

In the first report, an inference is drawn from the evidence of some witness, which wounds the honour of Mr. Hastings in the nicest part, and which, however warrantable from the evidence before them, is certainly unjust in point of fact. It hath already been very plainly proved, that Mr. Hastings was neither privy, nor accessary to the prosecution of Nundcomar; and I again repeat, that the *very same charge*, which he exhibits, was produced before the *very same Council*, that it was examined into by a special commission of *their* own appointment, that it was found to be false, and that the diary of these proceedings are amongst the records of the India House. This report was made two months ago, and it was the evidence, which had *then*, that the inference was drawn: the Committee are *now* examining witnesses, to prove the truth of this insinuation; but I should apprehend, you and all the world will agree, that the justice of this inference must stand, or fall, upon the evidence which was given at *that time*, and that an assertion, which is founded on the proof of a *prior act*, cannot be justified by a *subsequent declaration*. But since Mr. Hastings's character is *again* to appear at your tribunal, for acts which *have been* examined into, and of which he *hath been* most honourably acquitted, it is necessary you should be reminded of what has passed, as well as be informed by whom he is now accused.

The person whom the Committee have lately examined relative to this affair of Nundcomar, is a Mr. C—— G. who came a writer into your service in 1763, left it with a large fortune in 1767, and returned to it in 1774. This gentleman was the very man, who was appointed by General Clavering, Colonel Monson, and Mr. Francis, to seize on on all the houſehold papers and accounts of the Nabob from the year 1764 to 1772, in order that they might be delivered to Meſſrs. Maxwell, Anderſon, and Grant, for examination; as, from theſe papers, the identical charge now alluded to, and brought againſt Mr. Haſtings by Nundcomar, was to be eſtabliſhed. He was directed to diſmiſs the Nabob's mother from the office of regent, which ſhe held under the ſanction of the orders of the Court of Directors; he was empowered to remove her houſe and family, in groſs violation of the Oriental manners and cuſtoms; he was furniſhed with a military force to compel obedience to his orders; and he was authorized to ſeize, and confine any of the houſehold, who might require ſuch treatment. Armed with theſe extraordinary powers, he proceeded to the Nabob's palace, ſurrounded it with guards, and ſeized and confined the Begum's* principal eunuch, her confidential ſervant and chief adviſer. After having executed his orders in the moſt rigorous manner, after having tried every art to induce the Begum to accuſe Mr. Haſtings, and after every exertion of power and influence to criminate the Governor-General, nothing could be proved to his diſhonour, nor was his integrity in the ſmalleſt degree impeached.

Notwithſtanding the notoriety of theſe facts, the length of time which hath elapſed, and that both you and your Directors have honourably acquitted the Governor-General of theſe very charges, yet hath Mr. G—— intruded upon the public a renewal of that unjuſtifiable abuſe, which was a diſgrace to the men who firſt beſtowed it on the character of Mr. Haſtings: a character, fortunately for himſelf, free from every ſtain of corruption, and, happily for his friends, ſuch as they can ſtand forth to juſtify with credit and ſatiſfaction.

* Title of the Nabob's mother.

faction. At ſuch a time as this, when the ſtream of prejudice runs ſtrong againſt all orders of men who have been in India, the evidence of Mr. G—— might have been believed, if he had not luckily diſcovered a trait of his character, which muſt diſcredit it, even with partiality itſelf. He produced ſeveral ſealed papers to the Committee, which, he aſſured them, had never been opened, and which, he informed them, he had not delivered to the Council, becauſe he ſhould have incurred the general odium of the ſettlement by ſuch a diſcovery. He got poſſeſſion of this paper by virtue of the power which the Council had given him to ſeize on all the Nabob's accounts; conſequently, it was his duty to have delivered it to them. As to incurring the general odium of the ſettlement by ſuch a diſcovery, this cannot be the true motive of concealment, for he had done this long before by his conduct.

An INDEPENDENT PROPRIETOR.

LETTER IX.

THE reſult of the enquiry of the Secret Committee hath been an object of anxious expectation; and as the reſolutions to be formed on their report were likely to affect your rights at home and your affairs abroad, I have endeavoured to draw your attention to a ſubject, in which your intereſts are ſo eſſentially concerned.

Hitherto, we could only reaſon on circumſtances, as they occaſionally happened; and in their progreſſive courſe, we could

could only judge of their probable event. The enquiry hath now ended, the consequence is known, and the whole subject is fully before us. Let us consider it, for it greatly behoves us so to do, with strict attention and calm deliberation: let us divest ourselves, if possible, of prejudice, of passion, and partiality; let us not pin our faith upon the opinion of others, but form a judgment of our own; and let us convince the legislature, that we are capable both of understanding, and conducting our own affairs.

It hath already been made very clear, that the Secret and Select Committees have been inclined to coalesce in their votes of personal censure, and the nature of their appointments; and, notwithstanding the subjects of enquiry were so totally opposite, that it was not to be imagined their resolutions could possibly tend to the same point, yet it is now pretty plain, a similar end hath been pursued, although the means were apparently different; and this end seems to be *the removal of Mr. Hastings*; at least he is the principal figure in the piece, and therefore I shall take leave to consider him as the chief object in what relates to Bengal.

I do not believe that more pains were ever taken to depreciate a character, than have been used against Mr. Hastings, from the arrival in Bengal of General Clavering, Colonel Monson, and Mr. Francis, in the year 1774, until the present month of May, 1782, when Mr. Goring again appeared as his accuser, and was intruded on the Select Committee to bring forward a charge which hath been refuted these five years. The three gentlemen above-mentioned declared, "there was no species of peculation, of which the "Governor-General had not been guilty;" and they exerted all the influence of power to fix some charge upon him. He hath lately been represented as the abettor of what hath been called, a legal murder; and he hath been charged with having corrupted the integrity of a Judge. These are accusations of so heinous a nature, that could they have been justified, in any degree, Mr. Hastings would not have been the object of envy he now is. But happily for himself, his conduct hath been so free from all corruption, " he hath been so clear in his great office," that his merits plead for him in the strongest manner, and he now appears at your tribunal with an unblemished character; nor has all the influence of power, the rage of party, or the malice of his enemies, been able to bring the shadow of a proof to impeach his integrity.

The Secret Committee were so far from thinking his conduct had been influenced by interested views, that they expunged the term which conveyed so unjust an idea; and so far from being censured for dishonourable motives, that the resolutions of the House, which condemn his measures, apply only to what they deem political errors. With such incontestible proofs of an honest and able servant, as we have experienced in Mr. Hastings, let us not deprive ourselves of the services of such a man, for errors of judgment, or maxims of policy. His great abilities, his long experience, his respectable character amongst the natives, his profound knowledge of their government, language, and policy, his tried integrity, and his acknowledged services, are tests of merit, which we may safely appeal to, and by which we ought to be guided. In these we have a standard for our judgment, which is certain, and, therefore, as much superior to the fluctuating opinions of politicians, as experience is to speculation. I have the highest respect for the wisdom of many Members of the House of Commons, and particularly for that of the learned Lord, who brought forward the resolutions regarding your Government of Bengal; but they contain some positions which are as erroneous

as

as the meaſures they condemn, and they afford an additional proof to the many we had before, that all the knowledge which can be acquired by the moſt enlarged mind, in the courſe of a Seſſion of Parliament, is not ſufficient to eſtabliſh an infallible authority. On theſe reſolutions, however, the Houſe of Commons have come to one, which confirms the truth of an obſervation made by a member of that reſpectable body on another occaſion, viz.—"that our natural "diſpoſition leads all our enquiries rather to perſons than "things;"* for the only object that I can find out in this vote, is to deſire the Court of Directors to petition his Majeſty to remove Mr. Haſtings. This, I own, has a novel appearance, for your Court of Directors are competent to prefer ſuch a petition, without ſuch a recommendation. If it be a mere intimation from the Houſe of Commons of their deſire to your Directors, I humbly apprehend they can take no more notice of it than of a requeſt from the Treaſury Bench; and, I truſt, they are ſufficiently informed of their duty, to know, that whilſt they are bound by an act of the *whole* legiſlature, they cannot be controuled by only *one* branch of it. I do alſo conceive, that the Houſe have deſcended from their own dignity, by ſuch a recommendation. If Mr. Haſtings hath deſerved the cenſure of Parliament, the true conſtitutional mode of proceeding againſt him is by a bill. If he hath not done any thing to incur ſuch a puniſhment, it ſurely was beneath the dignity of that auguſt aſſembly, to vote a reſolution which was little better than a requeſt to the Court of Directors, and which they *alone* cannot enforce, if it ſhould be refuſed. If the legiſlature at large think proper to remove Mr. Haſtings, we muſt obey their power; but I hope we have ſpirit enough not to ſubmit either to threats or tricks.

AN INDEPENDENT PROPRIETOR.

* Vide Mr. Burke's ſpeech, on preſenting a plan for the better ſecurity of the independence of Parliament, &c. page 40, printed for Dodſley.

LETTER X.

THE important ſubject which hath ſo long excited our attention, is now upon the eve of determination; and Parliament will ſoon decide a queſtion, in regard to the government of Bengal, with which our rights and intereſts are ſo intimately connected, that it would be treachery to ourſelves to remain inactive.—The avowed principles of the Miniſtry are favourable to the claims of our charter; and if (as we have every reaſon to hope) they mean to guide their preſent conduct by their former ſentiments, we may aſſure ourſelves they will not act inconſiſtently with their profeſſions.—They will not ſay we have a right to manage our own affairs, and yet deny us the exerciſe of that right; they will not ſay we ought to appoint and remove our own ſervants, and yet do both themſelves; in ſhort, they will not invade our privileges and inſult our underſtanding.—But as we have had a recent inſtance, in the recall of a gallant Admiral in their own department, of the effects of prejudice and paſſion, we ought to be doubly fearful of the ſame conſequences in our affairs;—and as the example is ſo clearly connected with our ſituation, as to make us apprehenſive of its influence, it ought to warn us of our danger, and make us vigilant to avert it. —When we ſee that a warm imagination is ſoon heated into intemperance by intereſted tales and partial information, and that great talents are exerted to juſtify a miſconceived opinion; it ſhould teach us to guard againſt the fallacious

reaſoning

reaſoning of the one, and the ſpecious pretences of the other.

On theſe principles let us examine the conduct of the Secret Committee, and if we find that they have been miſled in their own judgment, or are likely to miſlead the judgment of others, it is a duty incumbent upon us to demand a hearing of the Legiſlature, and to aſſert our opinions in oppoſition to theirs. — The firſt idea which was entertained and propagated, was, that Mr. Haſtings was the author of the Mahratta war; and for this cauſe he was to be removed. — This opinion the Secret Committee ſoon deſtroyed by their report; and another was taken up, that he ſhould be removed for appointing the Chief Juſtice to the ſuperintendency of the Dewanny Addaulet. — This hath been laid aſide; and his conduct with the Vizir Sujah ud Dowlah, in tranſactions that happened eight years ago, and on which judgment hath been paſſed, was made the ſubject of cenſure. — In what manner, and how unworthy the dignity of Parliament, this attempt to remove him was made, I have already hinted at, and therefore will not repeat the diſgraceful circumſtance. After all theſe various expedients, another is going to be tried, the effect of which we ſhall ſoon know. But let the event of this meaſure be what it may, it ought not to alter our conduct. We have one decided rule to guide us, let Parliament act as it pleaſes; — and that is, to contend for the right of appointment and diſmiſſion of our own ſervants, or to relinquiſh the truſt altogether. As an individual of the ſociety, I can have no doubt of what I muſt loſe; and I am clear, that my firſt loſs in ſelling out will be leſs than what I muſt ſuffer, if the appointments which are talked of ſhould take place.

If there be any part of the conduct of Mr. Haſtings which the Legiſlature think ſo wrong, that he ought to be

removed,

removed, and the three Eſtates concur in ſuch a reſolution, we muſt, as in duty bound, ſubmit. If the charge be fairly brought, and impartially debated, as in ſuch a caſe we doubt not it will, the warmeſt advocates of Mr. Haſtings will not remonſtrate. And therefore as ſuch a reſolution muſt be the act of the united wiſdom of this nation, in which no intereſted views or paſſionate prejudices can have a ſhare; we may hope, that if the ſame wiſdom is exerted in appointments as well as diſmiſſion, the ſame care will be taken of your intereſts in the one as in the other. Report, however, gives us reaſon to entertain a different opinion; and as the report is currently circulated, and generally credited, we ought not to be regardleſs of it.

It hath been aſſerted very publicly, that Mr. Haſtings and the whole Council are to be recalled, and the perſons to be appointed in their room are to be Sir George Young, General Smith, Mr. D. Long, and Mr. William Burke. If this aſſertion ſhould be founded in truth, what are we to think of the motives of recalling Mr. Haſtings? and what recompenſe are we likely to find for the loſs of approved merit and tried integrity? I feel a repugnance to enter into invidious compariſons of perſonal merit; nor will I follow the unworthy example of drawing forced inferences from aſſumed principles; but I will not heſitate to declare, we deſerve to loſe our rights if we tacitly ſubmit to *any* ſet of men being forced upon us without our conſent: and I do alſo declare, that unleſs I ſee the moſt candid conduct purſued in the removal of Mr. Haſtings, and the moſt diſintereſted choice in a ſucceſſor, I never will believe that either the national intereſt or your's is conſulted by ſuch a change.

An INDEPENDENT PROPRIETOR.

LET-

LETTER XI.

So many motives conſpire to fix your attention on the proceedings of the Houſe of Commons relative to your affairs, that I cannot ſuppoſe the moſt indifferent perſon hath not maturely conſidered the conſequences of the reſolution, which paſſed on Tueſday laſt, on the motion of the Lord Advocate, and ſurely no perſon can have reflected on theſe conſequences, without being ſeriouſly alarmed—the queſtion is now no longer whether you ſhall have the appointment of your own ſervants, but whether one branch of the Legiſlature, ſhall do what belongs to the whole, and whether you ſhall interfere in the management of your own concerns ? It is now no longer a point, that affects merely the character and conduct of individuals in your ſervice ; it is become an argument of conſtitutional power, and of public concern, in which though your rights are immediately ſtruck at, yet thoſe of the whole community are remotely affected.

It was aſſerted in the Houſe of Commons that the Proprietors had nothing to do with the recal of Mr. Haſtings, but that it was a duty which appertained *ſolely* to the Court of Directors. The poſition as an abſolute one, is not ſtrictly true ; for though the law veſts this power in the Directors, yet they have never exerciſed the unconditional Letter of it, but always ſuppoſed the ſpirit of it meant to include the will of their conſtituents : conformably to this idea of its intention, they appealed to them, on a former occaſion, regarding Mr. Haſtings, on another regarding Lord Macartney and ſo they do on every important event.

The

The aſſertion therefore of the Court of Proprietors having nothing to do with this buſineſs, ſtanding in oppoſition to the remark of one of the members, is not juſtifiable in the unlimited ſenſe it was uſed, but, intending to convey the idea, that they ought not to be conſulted, it is a dangerous and improper doctrine.

If the Houſe of Commons mean to aſſert by their vote of Tueſday, that the Directors ought to recal Mr. Haſtings, that they have a right to expect obedience to ſuch a vote, and have a power to compel it, if it be refuſed; I humbly apprehend that ſuch an argument cannot be ſupported on conſtitutional principles; for if this be granted, they may paſs a vote to-morrow that we ought to divide only four per cent on our ſtock, which the Legiſlature limits at eight, and by the ſame parity of reaſoning, they may go on to vote, that we ought to have no excluſive privileges at all. I therefore repeat, that if the vote has this meaning, it is unconſtitutional, and not only the Proprietors, but every good ſubject ought to reſiſt it, for the increaſe of privilege is as dangerous as the increaſe of prerogative, and a juſt exerciſe of the three eſtates is, the true conſtitutional ballance of the Engliſh Government.

If the Houſe of Commons mean to aſſert that the conduct of the Governor General hath been ſo improper that he ought to be removed, they ſhould have ſtated the charge, and proceeded in a regular, conſtitutional manner by bill—but if they only mean to convey their ſenſe of what is the duty of the Directors, I muſt agree with an honourable member of their own, that they have brought themſelves into a ſituation, from which they cannot get out with credit, for I hope we have ſpirit enough, not to be dictated to on a matter, in which we have the ſole right of judging, a right that every maſter of a family in England enjoys,

a right

a right which is as sacred as our property, and which, if we suffer to be invaded, we deserve to lose. The right of Parliament, even to the territorial revenue is doubtful, but it is the only one in which the three estates have any pretence to interfere—Shall we then submit to the mandate of *only one* of these estates, and that too on a point in which they have clearly no power? Much, as hath been said of the omnipotence of Parliament, I do not believe that the warmest advocates for the republican part of our constitution will venture to assert, that the House of Commons *alone* have a power to vote any resolution which may affect the right of the subject—Shall their votes controul my household? Shall they dismiss my servants, because they disapprove my conduct? Shall I, as an individual, resist such a vote, and will you in your corporate capacity tamely submit to it? Shall every drunken porter in Westminster make the walls of St. Stephen ring with his cries for right, till the licentious sound is hailed the voice of God? And will so respectable a body as the East-India Company remain quiet spectators of an invasion of those privileges which it is the boast of an Englishman to preserve from the attack of either King, Lords, and Commons, whilst we have the exclusive right of trading to the East-Indies, and of ordering and managing the governments in that country? Let us exert that right, and suffer no interference. If the Legislature think proper to take away that right, let them do it, and take the responsibility and the risk along with it, but let us not have our servants garbled, and be made cyphers ourselves, to gratify the passions, the prejudices, or the interests of any set of men.

AN INDEPENDENT PROPRIETOR.

June 3, 1782.

LETTERS

TO THE

Right Honourable EDMUND BURKE.

LETTER I.

SIR,

IN the following letters, I do not mean intentionally to give you offence;—and as you are generally acknowledged to be a man of great urbanity, I hope my freedom will not displease you.

I was a witness on Wednesday evening, of the very unfortunate dilemma to which his Majesty's ministers were reduced, when Mr. Secretary Fox proposed a vote of thanks to that gallant veteran, Sir George Rodney—It was but a few days before, Sir, I saw you so remarkably active in bringing forward the St. Eustatia business, that you even quitted your favourite employment in the East-India Select Committee, to attend to it.—You best know, what motions would have been brought forward against Sir George Rodney if this glorious news had not arrived so opportunely.—I think, with Commodore Johnstone, that the brave Admiral's former services should have skreened him against such an attack, and against an abrupt recall, or rather removal from his command;—for, Sir, not all the ingenuity of your friend, Mr. Fox, will be able to persuade a sensible public, that a recall, however qualified, is not a disgrace

in

in time of war—as such, it was most assuredly, as you well know, intended.—I wish this, Sir, may induce you, and the rest of his Majesty's ministers, to be a *little more cautious* how you remove men in high and important commands from their stations. How the attempt, which was made on Thursday last, to remove Mr. Hastings, Sir Eyre Coote, and many others from their stations in India happened to fail, you perhaps can by this time account for. Be assured, Sir, the East-India Company will not willingly part with the services of such men at this most critical time, even though it should be intended to supply their places with Sir George Yonge, General Richard Smith, Mr. Dudley Long, and your relation, Mr. William Burke, the Agent to the Raja of Tanjore. In various resolutions of the Secret Committee the conduct of Mr. Hastings has been mentioned in the warmest terms of approbation.—The epithets, seasonable, wise, just, prudent, spirited, and proper, have been applied to various acts of the Supreme Council, which were proposed and carried by the casting voice of the Governor-General; and when the late resolutions were voted, upon which it was meant to effect his removal, had the Court of Directors obeyed the mandate, the only word which implied a doubt of Mr. Hastings's honour was agreed to be expunged.

ASIATICUS.

LETTER II.

THE very active part which you have taken against Mr. Hastings, since the commencement of the present session, and the ardour with which you still pursue the investigation of his conduct, induces me to offer a few more observations to your consideration. I do this, Sir, from a sincere belief that you are a man of honour and integrity; and that in the prosecution of this important object, you are biassed by no private views whatever. You have most unaccountably mistaken the real character of Mr. Hastings, and you deem it a point of duty, to procure his dismission from the government of Bengal. It has been proved, that the Mahratta war did not originate in Bengal. Mr. Hastings has been, it is true, censured for his conduct in the Rohilla war; but in commencing it, he was not biassed by any interested views, except for his constituents, who were relieved by it, from that state of bankruptcy, to which the politics of your friend, General Smith, had reduced them but a few years before. During the course of the war in the Carnatic, and the negociations with the Nizam, the conduct of Mr. Hastings is said to have been wise, seasonable, just, prudent, and spirited; taking, therefore, the whole of the subject into consideration, and seriously reflecting upon the consequences of removing such men as Mr. Hastings and Sir Eyre Coote, the Court of Directors certainly acted in conformity to the duty which they owe their constituents, when they refused to carry into effect that resolution, which you so strenuously, and I dare say, conscientiously supported. I own, Sir, I tread upon tender ground, when I presume to hazard opinions upon parliamentary questions. I wish not to give offence, and perhaps one branch of the Legislature may be competent to dictate to the East-India Company. If indeed your assertion was admitted, that the Directors wish to remove Mr. Hastings, all difficulties would cease; but I have every reason to believe, that a very great majority, both of the Directors and the Proprietors, would deem Mr. Hastings's recall at the present juncture to be the most unfortunate event

event that could befall them; and they have great confidence in Mr. Fox's declaration, to preſerve them in the exerciſe of their chartered rights.

Should the Governor-General be preſerved from the preſent attack, by the firmneſs of his conſtituents, who have repeatedly and honourably ſupported him againſt the whole force of government: you are, I am told, going to bring forward a charge, which muſt, as you think, moſt effectually cruſh him; I mean the buſineſs of Benares, which you repreſent to be ſtill more diſhonourable than Sir George Rodney's at St. Euſtatia. Your ſentiments upon Mr. Haſtings's conduct at Benares, you have explicitly declared in allplaces. The demand of money, which the Governor-General made upon the Raja, for the public ſervice, although it had the previous concurrence of every member of the Supreme Council, and was afterwards approved of by the Court of Directors, with the knowledge, as I preſume, of his Majeſty's late Miniſters, you term, upon all occaſions, a ſhameful robbery. The requiſition for cavalry, propoſed by Sir Eyre Coote, and aſſented to by the Council General, at a time of real danger, you aſſert to be a groſs violation of a ſolemn treaty; with what degree of juſtice, I ſhall take leave to explain in my next letter.

ASIATICUS.

LETTER III.

IN my last letter I presumed to point out to the Public the intemperate and unjustifiable heat with which your had invariably mentioned the unhappy affair at Benares. His Majesty's less prejudiced servants may perhaps entertain a very different opinion of it, when all the circumstances are fairly and candidly related to them. I know Mr. Hastings intimately, and I have seen a great deal of Mr. Burke in the last six months; nor will I allow, Sir, that your attention to those amiable qualities, justice and humanity, can exceed the Governor-General's.

By the treaty of Fyzabad in May 1775, the provinces of Benares and Gazypore were ceded to the East-India Company, by the present Vizier, Assoph ul Dowlah; they were at that time under the government of Cheyt Sing, a bastard son of the late Raja, Bulwant Sing, who had himself been confirmed and kept in the possession of these zemindaries by our influence. It was agreed that Cheyt Sing should hold them as a vassal of the East-India Company, precisely in the same manner as he had held them from his late sovereign the Vizier, to whom he had paid twenty-four lacks of rupees annually, and extra sums, in lieu of his quota of troops in time of war, agreeable to the constitution of the Empire. In my poor opinion, Sir, the question is simply this: Did we enter into an engagement with Cheyt Sing not to demand more than twenty-four lacks annually from him, let our exigencies be ever so great? If we did not, where was the injustice in our government,

of

of demanding from Cheyt Sing less than a moiety of the sums he had paid to Sujah Dowlah? That such requisitions were made by the superior power in Bengal, appears from an authority which, I am sure, you will not dispute. Your friend, Mr. Francis, has informed us, that Alliverdy Cawn, during the Mahratta invasion, applied to the Raja of Purnea for money on account of the extra expence of the war, who immediately gave him an order upon his banker for twelve lacks of rupees. The Raja stood precisely in the same situation with respect to Alliverdy Cawn, as Cheyt Sing did to our government when the demand was made upon him.

Our army continued upon a peace establishment from May 1775 to July 1778: the Raja, of course, paid his annual tribute, and no more. When we received advice of a rupture with France, it was thought necessary to raise several new corps, in all twelve battalions; and Cheyt Sing was very equitably called upon by the unanimous voice of the Supreme Council to contribute his proportion towards this additional expence. The annual sum was fixed at five lacks of rupees. Mr. Hastings was directed to write to the Raja, and to assure him he should not be subjected to this extra payment after the conclusion of the war. Cheyt Sing reluctantly complied with the requisition. The transaction was related tc the Court of Directors, who warmly approved of it. The second year, when there was a great probability of a change in administration in Bengal, Cheyt Sing positively refused to pay the money; but Sir Eyre Coote joining heartily with the Governor-General in support of the Company's authority, two battalions of seapoys were marched to his capital, and he then complied. The third year he again refused, and he accompanied the refusal by a declaration of his utter inability to pay

pay this ſum any longer. Whatever impreſſion the plea of inability may make in England, every man who has ſerved in Bengal muſt know the falſity of it. By the moſt moderate accounts, Cheyt Sing became poſſeſſed of two millions ſterling in ſpecie upon the death of his father. The annual revenues of Benares, &c. are 75 lacks of rupees; and the Raja paid us 24 lacks annually the firſt three years, and 29 lacks from 1778 to 1781. If, therefore, the demand is founded upon juſtice and precedent, the plea of inability will at once appear falſe and evaſive. The Raja had ſubmitted to demands infinitely more oppreſſive when he was a vaſſal to Sujah Dowlah. Captain Harper has told your Select Committee laſt year, that the Zemindar of Bernares furniſhed aſſiſtance to the Vizier in time of war, as a matter of courſe. In ſhort, I never heard the juſtice or the propriety of the demand called in queſtion by any man, at all converſant in the conſtitution of the Mogul empire: yet you, Sir, are pleaſed at all times, and in all places, to term it a ſhameful robbery. I believe you are candid enough to allow, that Mr. Haſtings or his friends have not profited by it. Sir, I applaud the goodneſs of your heart, but "you have paſſions that outſtrip the "wind." I hope, however, that the good ſenſe and moderation of the Engliſh nation, already rouſed by the violent perſecution of Sir George Rodney, (whoſe crime, I think, was robbery too in your idea) will prevent the Britiſh intereſts in India from falling a ſacrifice to them. Every reaſonable man, connected with the Company, is, I aſſure you, Sir, alarmed at your violence. To overſet, in one moment, all our eſtabliſhments in the Eaſt; to recall men who have retrieved our affairs, when reduced to the laſt diſtreſs, and when they were deemed deſperate both at home and abroad; appears, at the firſt view of it, to be abſolute

abſolute madneſs. Yet ſuch would have been the conſequences, if the motion which you ſo warmly ſupported on the 16th had been cordially received at the India-Houſe. It ran as follws: "That it is the duty of the Court of Directors to remove thoſe men, in whateuer degree employed, &c." including Mr. Haſtings, Sir Eyre Coote, Mr. Wheeler, and almoſt every civil and military ſervant of rank in India.

In my next letter I ſhall take leave to relate the unhappy conſequences of Cheyt Sing's intemperate and unconſtitutional reſiſtance.

ASIATICUS.

LETTER IV.

AS the unfortunate events which followed the refuſal of Cheyt Sing to comply with the demands of the Supreme Council, are as yet but imperfectly related, I ſhall forbear any farther comments upon them for the preſent, except to obſerve that the letter which Cheyt Sing wrote to Mr. Haſtings, was not a ſubmiſſive one, and that if it is compared with the former letters of that Rajah, or of Bulwaut Sing to former Governors, it will be found that Mr. Haſtings is juſtified in ſaying that it was offenſive both in ſtyle and ſubſtance.—The ſeverity which Mr. Haſtings exerciſed to the Rajah, a Zemindar dependent upon our government, was not greater than that which the Supreme Council authoriſed Mr. Goring to exerciſe in 1775, to a perſon of infinitely ſuperior rank — I mean the Begum, the widow of Meer Jaffier, and the guardian of the Nabob of Bengal.

Mr. Thomas Pitt has wisely said, that speculative opinions would ruin England.—If we carry your speculative opinions into practice, I am sure we have no claim to dominion in Asia; all our possessions there are usurpations undoubtedly; we gained India by the sword, and by the sword we must preserve it to this country. Not, Sir, that I am less inclined than yourself to justice, moderation, and good faith,—but we must sometimes submit to political expediency.—The gentlemen of the House of Commons, who ately voted against Mr. Hastings, have borne ample testimony to his integrity and splendid talents, — yet, instead of laying down a precise line for his conduct in future, they come to a resolution, that it is the duty of the Court of Directors to remove him, in order to deprive his constituents of the benefit of his talents hereafter. The unanswerable arguments of Commodore Johnstone had no weight with them, unless it were to draw from you that violent and unjustifiable declaration, that the Court of Proprietors had no voice in the removal of Mr. Hastings from the government of Bengal. I am a Proprietor, Sir, and no inconsiderable part of the small fortune I acquired abroad, is vested in East-India Stock. This declaration of your's, would, I confess, give me great alarm, were I not well assured that our present Directors will not attempt to move, in a matter of this importance, without consulting their constituents.---You have observed, Sir, that until Directors, Proprietors, and in short the whole nation shall get the better of avarice, we cannot hope for amendment. I confess this was an excellent sally, and the language is admirable from a man who has just jumped into the receipt of 4000l. a year, besides douceurs for the various branches of his family. But if we, who depend upon the receipt of our dividends for a subsistence, are to be deprived of it, in order to carry

carry your ſpeculative opinions into practice, what is to become of us?—I was, I confeſs, very well pleaſed with one declaration of your's, that no man who had been ſuſpected of peculation abroad, *or convicted of bribery at home*, ſhould fill a ſtation of importance in India; I am now therefore perfectly convinced, that ſome gentlemen who have been publicly talked of for the government of Bengal, or as members of that adminiſtration, may give up all hopes of ſucceſs—ſince they certainly come within that deſcription of men, whom you have ſo juſtly pronounced to be improper perſons to fill ſuch honourable and reſpectable ſtations.

ASIATICUS.

To the PROPRIETORS of EAST-INDIA STOCK,

GENTLEMEN,

IT cannot but be matter of ſurprize to every impartial obſerver of public affairs, that the labours of two moſt reſpectable Committees of the Houſe of Commons, exerted through many months with unabated ardour, ſhould appear at laſt to have hardly any other object, than the removal of a Governor, or Governors, from ſome of the Eaſt-India Company's ſettlements. — The aſtoniſhment muſt be greatly increaſed, when it is remarked, that ſo much energy and ſuch powerful engines, have not yet proved equal to the attempt. The taſk of affixing the ſtigma of culpability on an unblemiſhed character becomes every day more difficult. Brilliancy of imagination, and fertility of argument, have ruſhed like a torrent through the Houſe: ſhift, ſubterfuge, miſrepreſentation, and quibble, have almoſt carried our underſtandings by ſtorm without doors; and yet the grand affair is ſtill incomplete. — The delay of a week, of a day, of an hour, is felt on both ſides — but with very different ſenſations. The friends of the Governor-General are convinced that the integrity, the wiſdom, the humanity of that great man will, and muſt, ſooner or later, be univerſally acknowledged, — and they flatter themſelves, that every day gains them a new proſelyte; hence their wiſh to procraſtinate. Internal conviction is no leſs powerful on the oppoſite party, and actuates on their fears in a more than equal proportion. As the eyes of people gradually open, the private or partial, or unworthy views of certain intereſted men may at length glare out in their true colours; and the moſt complying ſpirits may in time grow tired of bowing to the gauze of patriotiſm, whenever it fails to conceal the deformity of perſonal ambition. Hence their almoſt indecent urgency of diſpatch.

The two Committees, which for a long time were thought hoſtile to each other, have now joined iſſue, and ſeemed determined to keep up the ball of cenſure, by a perpetual repercuſſion of attack. The Select Committee, in examining the proceedings of the Court of Judicature in Bengal, diſcovers Mr. Haſtings to have tampered with the independence and integrity of a Judge. Scarce has the accuſation gone forth, when the neceſſity and policy of the meaſure in queſtion is ſo accurately diſplayed, as to convert it to a moſt laudable effort for the public tranquillity. The learned Chairman from the Secret Committee brings up forty-four reſolutions, ſome of fact, and many otherwiſe; but with no other oſtenſible object than that of criminating Mr. Haſtings in his political department. Before he can get them through the Houſe, their purport is canvaſſed without doors, and the principle of moſt of them refuted, from the very text whence they were drawn. The Select Committee then endeavour to mould into ſome ſhape an ill-digeſted maſs of old and long-refuted charges, fiſhed up afreſh from *one Mr. Goring*. This ſtubborn embryo has not yet acquired the form or conſiſtency of a Report; but whenever it ſhall appear, it will certainly undergo ſome diſcuſſions, not quite palatable to its parents and god-fathers. In the mean time, the game is held out by an artificial diſpoſition of the imperfect fragments of a mutilated ſtory from Benares. This arrived too late to conſtitute a component ſection of the ſixth Report from the Secret Committee; but too opportunely, not to become a moſt valuable *rider*, or after-piece. The grand battery of forty-four reſolutions was already opened, but the laſt piece was now to be new charged,

charged, and levelled, like that of a rifleman, point blank at the enemy's General: great part of its force lay in its precipitancy. On Monday, a new report and motion respecting the Benares business is promised in the House of Commons for the next Tuesday; — the publisher takes up the whole of Monday night to print it; — on Tuesday, out it comes, as a fresh Report, (being nothing but an abridged and avowedly imperfect statement of the behaviour of Rajah Cheyt Sing, Zemindar of Benares, in a short letter from Mr. Hastings, and another short letter from the Council-General of Bengal) and this phantom of intelligence (as if it were a full proof of delinquency) is followed up with a direct proposal for the recall of Governor-General Hastings, by a modification of the forty-fourth resolution. Thus is the Benares business, which every builder, who knew any thing of Asiatic architecture, would reject as a worthless pebble, become the corner-stone in the edifice of accusation. In plain terms, of all the various charges which have been exhibited against Mr. Hastings, his dispute with Cheyt Sing must seem to every man, acquainted with the principles and politics of Indian governments, by much the most frivolous. All the pains which have been taken by a great Patriot both in public and in private, to brand it with the stigma of a *robbery*, have been thrown away, — no less than another great Patriot's ridiculous renunciation of his share in the Company's dividend. Not a man who heard this imperious and disappointed bashaw in his ostentatious pretences to self-denial, and *pecuniary self-denial*, but laughed at him: none who knew any thing of his practices in India, or who have observed his egregious vanity and profusion, since his last return, (and which of us has not observed it?) but were disgusted at the nauseous improbability. The spot for the fresh attack was therefore very wisely shifted. The

station

ſtation of '*robbery*,' beſides being untenable, belonged to the other Committee; and appearances were much better preſerved, by breaking ground on the ſubject of Cheyt Sing's letter, by Mr. Haſtings termed 'diſreſpectful and unſatisfactory,' by the learned Lord 'an acknowledgment of ſlavery.' Mr. Haſtings has been upwards of thirty years in India; he has on many important occaſions acted as Perſian interpreter, while reſident at the Durbar, under that great and good man, Governor Henry Vanſittart: he is an equal proficient, and an experienced maſter in the dialects of poetical compoſition, and of political negociation in India. Shall he go to ſchool to the Lord Advocate to be taught the ſtyle and implication of a Perſian letter? Does the learned Lord underſtand an iota of its phraſeology, or even of its character? Or does he pretend to the ſame intuitive knowledge and literary ſecond-ſight as hath enabled another great genius to diſcern at a glance, and to decide *ex cathedra*, whether a tranſlated letter were originally written in Engliſh or in Perſian? Such gigantic ſcholars carry before them the whole Encyclopedia of learning as eaſily as they carry the Houſe of Commons! After all, it is more than probable, that if all the perſons now in London, who have ever been in India, and who are converſant in the politics of that country, were called to the bar of that Houſe, they would teſtify their cleareſt ſenſe of the improper ſtyle and diſreſpectful inſinuations applied in Cheyt Sing's letter; at leaſt it would be worth while to examine them. The acknowledgment of ſlavery implies about as much as if I ſhould ſubſcribe myſelf, 'your moſt obedient humble ſervant,' to the Lord Advocate.

Granting, however, for a moment, that the learned Lord's poſition with reſpect to the ſtyle of Cheyt Sing's letter, be admiſſible, he hath introduced a circumſtance (if Mr. Woodfall

Woodfall has done juſtice to his ſpeech of Tueſday) which, when rightly ſtated, would totally change the nature of the queſtion. " This letter," (ſays the noble Lord) " ſtated " the payment of a tribute which the Governor had no " right to demand, the impaling of ſeveral perſons; and " concluded with an acknowledgment of ſlavery; yet this " letter was termed inſolent by the Governor, and *accounted* " *a cauſe for war.*" Under an idea that the Morning Chronicle muſt have imperfectly ſtated the learned Lord's ſpeech, I cannot heſitate to pronounce poſitively, that *no ſuch cauſe for war was ever accounted to exiſt.* The letter was termed diſreſpectful, and ſo it undoubtedly is,—and more diſreſpectful, from the taunting, ironical acknowledgment of ſlavery. It is alſo extremely prevaricating and unſatisfactory, (which ſurely the learned Lord will not deny) and was therefore deemed by the Governor a cauſe for putting the Rajah under an arreſt. The ſubſequent maſſacre of two companies of ſeapoys, and three European officers, by the contrivance and orders of Cheyt Sing, was deemed by the Governor, and muſt be deemed by all the world, a very ſufficient cauſe for war; if the learned Lord ſhall chooſe to ſtile by the denomination of war, a ſpecies of hoſtilities which began in treaſon, and ended in rebellion. Cheyt Sing was not an independent Prince; he owed the fealty of military ſervice, or pecuniary commutation, to his paramount, the Company, or the Company's repreſentative. His reſiſtance was rebellion, his downfal a judicial puniſhment, not a hoſtile overthrow. It appears in evidence from Captain Harper, that he was forced, under the exigencies of ſtate, to furniſh troops to his late ſovereign, Sujah ud Dowla. Immediate loſs of fortune and life would then have followed the preſumption of a refuſal; and the conſtitution of the Mogul Empire would have juſtified the execution. The

Company

Company is now in the place of Sujah Dowla; the Company's general lenity is an aggravation to the Rajah's insolence. Should he now be restored to power, it will be an encouragement, a commission to every native of Hindostan to revolt from our dominion, and a pledge for his security under a defeat; on this plea the whole affair turns. Had Cheyt Sing obeyed his arrest quietly, or rather had he given orders for the payment of what the Governor-General (by the feudal tenure of Cheyt Sing's Zemindary, and under sanction of the Company's assent) had a strict and clear right to demand; had he conformed with sincerity to the necessary regulations proposed for his conduct, the matter would have been fully settled in three days, to the satisfaction of all parties. What construction shall we now put on Cheyt Sing's inexhaustible pleas of inability, when we find, (as advices received two days ago specify) that 120 lacks from his treasures have been already remitted to Calcutta?

But it is now time to close my letter; I cannot do it without congratulating our self-inspired scholars on their knowledge of Persian, as well as on some more of their triumphs. But I must beg leave to observe, that it will require an additional degree of dexterity, to convince an independent Court of Proprietors of the necessity of Mr. Hasting's recall. The gentlemen know that I, as a mere private gentleman, should laugh at them, if they were to pretend, by a vote of the House of Commons, to urge the expediency of merely removing my footman from one garret to the next: much more, that the most powerful and most extensive corporate body in this kingdom, may, and can, and ought to set at defiance every attempt of this single branch of the Legislature, to domineer over their resolutions, or to interfere in the internal management of their domeſtic concerns. The very idea is an innovation on the principles of the Britiſh Conſtitution. If the Houſe of Commons chooſe to recall Mr. Haſtings, or any other man, let it be done fairly and with effect *by bill*, and conſent of all the branches of the Legiſlature. I never heard that the Houſe of Commons had any excluſive power or privilege of this kind. If the Eaſt-India Company be diſſatisfied with the conduct of a Governor of their own, they need not ſolicit the aſſiſtance of the Commons; they are competent to do it in a legal and conſtitutional mode, nor do they want advice. The Court of Proprietors will feel collectively, what each member feels as an individual, that the value of their ſtock depends on the abilities and integrity of their delegated ſervants. If there exiſts a man more fit for the high truſt of Governor-General than Mr. Haſtings is, their own intereſt will make them quick-ſighted to the diſcovery. But *that man* is yet to ſeek, and will, I fear, be long unfound, to the unſpeakable mortification of

A PROPIETOR.

THE END.

THOUGHTS.

CHEYT SING's preparations for revolt from the government of Bengal, will be found to have anticipated the time of the Governor General's departure from Calcutta. Acknowledgments of ſlavery in his mouth, but treaſon and rebellion in his heart. His expreſſions were never ſo ſervile and ſubmiſſive, as after his arreſt, at the very moment when two companies of Seapoys, with three European officers, were going to be butchered under his eye, and by his immediate orders.

What opnion had Cheyt Sing entertained of the Company's right, to demand additional tribute or auxiliary troops on the event of a war? Read his letters—Do they indicate a doubt of the legality, or propriety, or even moderation of the demand? No, they teem with pleas of inability only—ſuch as the cuſtom of all the fœdal tenants, or tributary Zemindars, throughout Hindoſtan, renders fully warrantable. But he well knew the obligation, and hoped, perhaps, by his perpetual excuſes, to tire out the patience of his maſters, or to extort from their compaſſion ſome abatement of the aſſeſſment. The conſtant example of Shuja ud Dowlah's valid and enforced claims on his father, and the eſtabliſhed practice of all India, could not leave a ſhadow of doubt on his mind reſpecting the full competency of the Council-General's powers.

The Houſe of Commons comes to reſolutions for the neceſſity of political forbearance in India, and for eſtabliſhing the character of Britiſh moderation, good faith, &c. on a renunciation of all conqueſts, at the very moment that the members and the public are warmly congratulating each other on the repeated ſucceſs of our arms over Hyder Ally and the Mahrattas.

What will the natives of India think of Britiſh moderation, when they ſee us thruſting out every European nation by turns from the Aſiatic continent. They have been accuſtomed, indeed, to ſee us quarrel with the French, and have been frequent witneſſes to our ſuperiority—but how will they digeſt our treatment of the Dutch, who have proceeded on the uniform ſyſtem of neutrality for more than 150 years, and have conſtantly afforded an aſylum for all parties, natives or Europeans, in all the ſtruggles and revolutions which have happened ſince that period? All India can bear ſtrong teſtimony to the peaceable behaviour and unſuſpecting tranquillity of the Dutch in that quarter; yet we ſeize their towns, plunder their property, and impriſon their perſons, without ſo much as a declaration of war—Such vigorous meaſures will probably inſure the ſubmiſſion of our Indian ſubjects, but will hardly inſpire them with a lofty opinion of our moderation. Aſia has been ever ruled by the ſword, and is now too far advanced in years to taſte any other principles of government.

Rodney's

Rodney's recall was constitutional; it originated with the ministry, in whom lodged the executive power. Their *right* was never questioned, but the expediency of the measure has been much disputed. See how Mr. Fox reprobates the idea of an interference on the part of the House of Commons.—The Court of Directors holds the same relation to Mr. Hastings, with that of administration to Lord Rodney—nay more, a precise mode for removing the Governor-General is expressly provided by law, and the power vested in the Court of Directors by act of Parliament; where then is there room for the interference of the House of Commons? The line is at least as accurately drawn in the one case as in the other.

Many are Mr. Hastings's friends, and his enemies are many; but they both join in admitting his singlar integrity, and all acknowledge the difficulty of finding an adequate substitute for him in the government of Bengal. Not one of them but is free to declare the insufficiency of each of those gentlemen, whose names are whispered as candidates for the succession. Nothing is so easy as to point out what men are *unfit* for the office and why. The doctrine of the day is, that the Court of Directors is competent to remove Mr. Hastings without any communication with the Court of Proprietors. The formal letter of the law, indeed, does thus word the position—but yet does not warrant the conclusion: For by the same law, a general controuling power over the Court of Directors, is lodged in that of the Proprietors; and the reason of the thing makes it evident, if law be the perfection of reason, as I have heard. For the Court of Directors is, in fact, nothing but a committee of Proprietors, a quorum for the dispatch of business. They are the first delegated servants of the Company, and as such, are accountable to the whole body for their conduct. Do not the Proprietors frequently exert the right of rescinding the resolutions of the Directors, and do they not after all possess that right.

The ministry now contend that to them belong the political measures of the Company; they claim all the power, and all the responsibility. The Chairman of the Court of Directors on Tuesday the 18th of May last, standing up in his place in the House of Commons, acknowledged the justice of the claim, and renounced as the head official servant of the Company all political responsibility whatsoever. Where is now the Company's independence?

No books, no theory, no recluse speculation will ever fit a man for the office of Governor General of Bengal; he must have abilities political and commercial, knowledge, local and experimental, acquired by long residence on the spot; he must not be inflexibly wedded to one undeviating mode of action, nor bigotted to any particular system of legislation He should have judgment to discern where to temporize, and resolution to dare the invidious consequences of a great action. In short, he should know how to relax in every thing but integrity. The duty is of so mixed a nature, and comprehends so many

many different relations with respect to Europe and India, it is so difficult to hold the balance in such a manner between them, as that what is serviceable to the one may not injure the other, that it is rather more extraordinary a man should ever have been found to hold the office with success during seven years, and more critical than the last, than that the difficulty of removing him should now be the cause of a thousand intrigues and machinations within and without doors. Were not the experiment too seriously dangerous for the Company and the nation, I should be happy to see one of these Governors-by-intuition put precisely into Mr. Hastings's place for a few years. I would only request to insert one article in the treaty; that Mr. Hastings should previously stipulate, that he will not refuse after three or four years, to return once more and be the salvation of India.

Every man presumes to demand the government, particularly if he has ever been in India; if he have but birth, or impudence, or a shattered fortune, he thinks himself entitled and well qualified for the post; the Courts of Directors and Proprietors may, if they choose it, place the alternative of the Company's prosperity and perdition in such hands. But they would not employ a shoemaker who had not served a seven years apprenticeship. The time may come, when Indian affairs shall be so methodically and systematically arranged (principally by Mr. Hastings's long and successful labours) that any man of common understanding and common honesty may manage them: at present nothing less than uncommon talents and uncommon integrity will do the business. India is not yet ripe for your S——s and F——s. We must now have a man who can resist strong temptations, and who has other modes of shewing his contempt of money, than by squandering in every vain and profligate extravagance immense sums acquired with a very suspicious rapidity.

No man is blamed as a public character, for dedicating some portion of his time to his private affairs: It is even allowable for him to find the means of connecting his own personal interest with his official duty. But he only is truly *great* who has no time for himself, and who never admits *self-consideration* to go hand in hand with the business of the State. The illustrious Vasco de Gama, who first planted the Portuguese power in India, brought no acquired wealth from thence, but the first China orange-tree, a noble inheritance which he bequeathed to the European world. Mr. Hastings, after having served thirty years in India, without a vice to gratify, or an extravagance to feed, is not now worth half the salary he has received by act of parliament for the last seven years. Mr. Francis, who has served somewhat less than those seven years, and with two-fifths of the appointment, is probably the richer man.

Mr. Hastings has acquired friends among those who know him by his great personal affability; among those who know him not, by important actions. His character and his conduct only preserve their friendship, for he has never gratified any of them at the public expence.

pence. Even the regular road of promotion in the routine of the service hardly avails them; so cautious is he of furnishing matter for accusations, that he is unbiassed by private partiality in the line of his public conduct: for the same reason those who have acted with the most declared enmity towards him, have been permitted to enjoy every advantage procured for them by their less scrupulous patrons, that he might not seem actuated by a spirit of revenge. Look round among the Company's servants now at home. Those who exclaim the loudest against Mr. Hastings's politics, and are mingling *fas atque nefas* to supplant him, wallow in wealth obtained under his very nose. They are, indeed, at once the accusers and the proofs of his misconduct. Their acquisitions are a reproach to Mr. Hastings. The few who are called his friends cannot at best rise above an humble mediocrity, and the greater part are now soliciting to return to India for bread.

Lord Clive, with all his merit, had not the essential qualifications of a civil governor. Military habits never sit well upon commercial principles. His own glory and the Company's advantages were the result of the well exercised talents of a soldier. With a warmth of genius, a promptitude of decision, and a vigour of execution unknown in the annals of India, he was unfit for the tormenting details and formal minutiæ of a peaceful administration, founded on a commercial basis. Mr. Hastings makes no pretensions to military merit, and yet he has never embarked in war but with a decisive success. Our armies have fought and conquered as often under his auspices as under Clive's command, and that with the disadvantage of a frequent change of generals. In the mean time civil arrangements have occupied much the greater portion of his time, and are infinitely the most valuable part of his administration. His œconomical plans have saved the Company immense sums. His political negociations have procured them *de novo* much more. His encouragements have added to the mercantile gains of his employers, and his regulations to the prosperity of the state. In his time new manufactures have been brought to maturity, and the old to perfection: Mines of coal, iron, &c. have been worked to advantage; commerce and internal intercourse have been promoted, by rendering navigable many canals that were obstructed by sands and by new cuts where none before existed. The native languages of India have been printed on the spot, and the door thus shut on the general prosperity of the natives to forgery, without the necessity of a sanguinary penal law. Translations have been procured of all the most respectable and fundamental law treatises either in the Mahometan or Hindoo system, for the general direction of all judges in the country courts, and to the exceeding satisfaction of all the inhabitants. In short, industry has been infinitely encouraged, internal tranquillity effectually secured, and the commerce, the politics, the legislature, and the finances of Bengal improved within the last seven years, to so wonderful a pitch, that at present the very existence of the British empire seems on all hands to be allowed to depend on the preservation of her Asiatic influence,

LETTER V.

To the Right Hon. EDMUND BURKE.

SIR,

THE Swallow's packets being in part arrived, I ſhall take leave to renew my correſpondence with you. You will ſoon receive the moſt ample and convincing proofs, that Cheyt Sing had entered into an engagement with the mother of the Vizier, and the Raja of Goorucpoor, to excite commotions in Oude, that he had promiſed a conſiderable ſum of money to Futty Shaw, to invade the province of Bahar; and that he had taken meaſures to aſſert his own independence, by collecting a very conſiderable army, and a train of artillery, with ammunition and military ſtores of every kind, and in great quantities, in the neighbourhood of Benares, previous to the Governor General's departure from Calcutta.——Mr. Haſtings has indeed been culpable, not for ſeverity to Cheyt Sing, but for a neglect of the repeated intelligence which had been ſent him, of the preparation and hoſtile deſigns of the Raja.

The Chairman of the Court of Directors, Mr. Gregory, came forward at the laſt general Court of Proprietors, and acknowledged that Mr. Haſtings had not wilfully detained in Bengal, thoſe diſpatches which ought to have been received by the Belmont. It appears by a note from the Secretary at Calcutta, that the direction of that packet having been accidentally torn of, it was returned to Fort William. With what violence did both Mr. Gregory and yourſelf dwell upon this ſubject in the Houſe of Commons, a few days ago!——with what contemptuous indifference did you treat Mr. Barwell's honeſt attempts to explain this matter to the Houſe! How did you in your Select Committee reject the aſſurances which Major Scott ventured to give you, that Mr. Haſtings was ſuperior to the low, paltry trick of with-holding any public act of his government, from the knowledge of the Directors? —Besides, in the instance alluded to, it would argue folly as well as indiscretion. Mr. Hastings had made a reform in the mode of collecting the revenues of Bengal, which would naturally subject him to much personal odium; was it to be supposed, therefore, that he would intentionally with-hold his reasons for adopting a measure which, however beneficial to the Company, was destructive to the interest of several individuals? Neither this reasoning, nor the readiness of Major Scott, to furnish your Committee with copies of every paper in his possession, could conquer your prejudices: but I flatter myself, Sir, as the matter is now fully explained, you will join with Mr. Gregory, in procuring the Forty-Second resolution to be rescinded from the votes of the House of Commons; and if your report on the revenues of Bengal, confessedly drawn up from imperfect materials, is not yet completed, let me advise you now to compare Mr. Hastings's plan with its effects.

Mr. Wheler and Mr. Macpherson have spoke warmly of it in their public letter.

I have, I confess, Sir, been much at a loss to account for that more than common industry, which you have employed in your investigation of Mr. Hastings's conduct.—Pardon me, Sir, for presuming to observe to you, that I think you rather stepped beyond the bounds of moderation, when you brought forward Mr. Goring to the Select Committee, to give evidence upon a transaction, which happened in Bengal in the year 1775, and had been finally determined upon by the Directors, and the Court of Proprietors, in 1776.—Perhaps I may have formed an erroneous judgment of your motives, but I cannot help thinking Mr. Hastings has offended you by an opinion, which he has freely given, respecting the Raja of Tanjore, to whom, if I am rightly informed, your cousin, Mr. William Burke, is an avowed agent, with a fixed salary of eight thousand pounds per annum. Let me, Sir, take this opportunity of congratulating you upon his safe arrival at the capital of the Raja, and upon the gracious reception he met with. I presume Mr. William Burke did not take two trips over land to India, merely for the purpose of succouring "Virtue in Distress."—What Mr Hastings's opinion, respecting the claims of the Raja of Tanjore, and the Nabob of the Carnatic, has invariably been, shall be the subject of my next letter.

June 10, 1782. ASIATICUS.

LETTER

LETTER VI.

To the Right Hon. EDMUND BURKE.

SIR, June 12, 1782.

I HAVE presumed to hint that the principal cause of your persecution of Mr. Hastings, is the opinion which that gentleman has unfortunately entertained respecting the rights of the Rajah of Tanjore. The Governor General has unreservedly declared, that Tanjore being a dependency of the Carnatic, the Nabob, or the representatives of the East India Company at Fort St. George, with his consent, have an undoubted right, in the present distressed state of the Carnatic, to insist upon the Rajah contributing the amount of his revenues to the public service, after reserving the necessary sums for his private expences. This opinion is surely founded upon reason, justice, and common sense. I shall not quote all the unanswerable arguments which Mr. Hastings has urged in support of his opinion; let it suffice in this place to observe, that the Governor General could have no private views to gratify, when he assented to the proposal of the select committee of Fort St. George, to compel the Rajah of Tanjore to contribute as far as he could to the support of the present arduous contest.

You will pardon me, I hope, Sir, for observing, that where the interests of the Nabob of the Carnatic, and the Rajah of Tanjore are in question, you cannot, nay you ought not to be considered as an unbiassed, and an impartial judge.

In the year 1777, your cousin, Mr. William Burke, accepted the appointment of agent to the Rajah of Tanjore, with a salary annexed to it, as I am told, of 8000l. per annum. He arrived at Madras in September 1777, made a short stay there, returned to England, and last year made a second over land trip to Tanjore, where he has met with a most distinguished reception. Whether the Nabob has been ill used by the Rajah, or the Rajah by the Nabob, or (which I believe to be the true ſtate of the caſe) that both have been extremely ill uſed by the Court of Directors, it is not my buſineſs to enquire; let impartial men determine the point in diſpute. You certainly are a party in the buſineſs, in as much as you muſt naturally be anxious for the ſucceſs of your couſin, the agent.

Let me intreat you, Sir, to be extremely cautious how you preſs the chairman of the Court of Directors, to ſend orders to Fort St. George, for overturning any regulations, which may have been formed for bringing a part of the revenues of Tanjore into our treaſury, or a proportion of its grain into our magazines. That gallant officer, Sir Eyre Coote, has been prevented, by a want of proviſions, from purſuing his victories. This is not a time for weakening the hands of our governments in India: It would ſurely be better at once to give up the conteſt, and to quit the Carnatic, if when that country is totally exhauſted, the Nabob and the Company are not allowed to call upon a dependent Zemindar for aſſiſtance, without a violation of our national character for juſtice, moderation, and good faith.

May I, Sir, preſume juſt to touch upon a ſubject nearer home. It is confidently aſſerted, but I profeſs I can hardly give credit to the aſſertion, that your relation Mr. William Burke has lately been appointed pay maſter or commiſſary to his Majeſty's forces in India, with a ſalary of 1900l. per annum. This poſt, I can aſſure you, Sir, is as completely uſeleſs as any one of thoſe which, in your œconomical bill, you propoſe to reform; nay, were it neceſſary at all, I humbly conceive, Mr. William Burke's Tanjore agency would incapacitate him, from performing the duties of it. As a proprietor of the Eaſt-India ſtock, I do hope the Company will not be ſaddled with the payment of this uſeleſs office; and as a Britiſh ſubject, anxious to ſee that plan of reform take place, which has been ſo faithfully promiſed, I cannot but lament, that a new poſt ſhould be created, to add another two thouſand pounds to the annual income of your family. I muſt do you the juſtice to ſay, Sir, that conſidering the ſhort time you have been a miniſter, you have not been inattentive to your own, as well as to the national concerns.

ASIATICUS.

LETTER

LETTER VII.

To the Right Hon. EDMUND BURKE, *and Brigadier-General* RICHARD SMITH.

I IMAGINE your speeches upon Mr. Dempster's motion, on Thursday, must have been grossly misrepresented in the public papers. Did you really say, Gentlemen, that Sir Elijah Impey's refusal to accept a salary to the appointment of the Adaulet, did not tend at all to his exculpation? and that probably his refusal was owing to his knowledge of your Committee having been instituted? To the last I can only declare, that when the salary was offered to Sir Elijah Impey, no intelligence whatever, respecting your Committee, had arrived in India. If I were to judge, Gentlemen, from the pains which both of you took to draw from Major Scott a declaration, that Sir Elijah Impey had accepted a salary, I should suppose, you deemed it of some consequence to establish that fact. Mr. Burke examined him closely for above three hours, upon that single point. I confess, when I consider the very candid manner in which Major Scott answered every question that was put to him, and the eager inclination he shewed to give your Committee every information in his power, I could not help being surprised that you should examine him so much in the style of an Old Bailey witness; but when I saw a slip of paper upon the table of your Committee, with words to the following purport upon it, and in a hand I well knew, my astonishment vanished:—"By a private letter from Calcutta, "of the 9th of January 1781, it appears, that the business "of the salary was done." Considering the *very respectable quarter* from which this information came, I no longer wondered that you questioned Major Scott so closely. From that time to the present, however, I understood, and I am sure the report (which by Generel Smith's account is to immortalize Mr. Burke) tends to prove it, that the acceptance of the salary, which is taken for granted, was the criminal part of Sir Elijah's conduct. I do most firmly believe, that when the House voted an address to the King, to recal Sir Elijah Impey, they conceived he had accepted a salary, and that if the evidence which has now been produced, had then appeared, no such vote would have passed; but I may be mistaken—Governor

nor Johnstone is said, by the papers, to have accused you of shameful partiality, and to have added, that when you wanted evidence to criminate a man, you were ready enough to search records, letters, &c. Far be it from me to take such a liberty with men of your exalted stations; but allow me to relate a plain fact, in plain language.

Three days after the arrival of General Clavering, Colonel Monson, and Mr. Francis, in Calcutta, they attacked the public measures of Mr. Hastings. In three months they told the Directors, that there was no species of peculation of which the Governor General, had not been guilty, and that, in less than thirty months, he had amassed a fortune of 400,000l. Mr. Goring was deputed to Moorshedabad to procure such proofs as might justify these assertions. None, however, were obtained. The matter was fully examined by the Court of Directors and Proprietors in 1776, when the whole force of government was exerted to remove Mr. Hastings. At that time he was supported by the late Marquis of Rockingham and Mr. Burke's particular friends, but he owed his preservation to the weight of his own personal character. All good men lamented the violence to which two most respectable persons, General Clavering and Colonel Monson, had been drawn, and this business lay dormant from 1776 until the other day, when Mr. Burke thought proper to bring Mr. Goring before the Select Committee. I hope the world, will one time or other, be favored with an account of his examination, and Major Scott's remarks upon it; but if it does not appear in the next Report, I shall take leave to relate it as accurately as I can from memory, for I attended to the whole examination very closely. Perhaps Governor Johnstone might have alluded to this transaction; I shall not however, presume to determine, whether bringing Mr. Goring before a committee of the House of Commons in 1782, to examine him upon points that the East India Company had pronounced judgment upon in 1776, did not look very like personal persecution. I must do General Smith the justice to say, that he was indisposed when Mr. Goring first appeared before the Committee, and that I believe he disapproved of it.

Let it be remembered that on that remarkable day, when the House of Commons resolved "that it was the duty of "the Court of Directors to remove Mr. Hastings, &c." not a member spoke to the resolution, without declaring that the abilities of the Governor General were of the most splendid kind, and his integrity unquestionable.

July 15, 1782. ASIATICUS.

For the MORNING HERALD.

LETTER VIII.

Mr. EDITOR, *August* 9, 1782.

IN a late paper it was asserteo, that the idea of removing Mr. Hastings, and of punishing East-India delinquents, was given up by Lord Shelburne. Upon reading this paragraph, I could not restrain my inclination to send you a connected narrative of the treatment which Mr Hastings has met with from the House of Commons, and an infatuated majority of the Court of Directors. His conduct has been arraigned by two Committees, who certainly were formed for purposes far different. The first, the Select Committee, met last year, to take the state of the judicature in Bengal under their consideration; at the commencement of the late session, their powers were extended, and they were directed to enquire, by what means our valuable possessions in Bengal, &c. could be best governed. Far be it from me, Sir, to arraign their proceedings: I do assert, that no man living can be more anxious than Mr. Hastings is, to have his conduct fairly and fully investigated: whether the investigation which the Select Committee entered into was a candid one, let their reports determine: Commodore Johnstone has publicly accused the Committee of gross and scandalous partiality——the charge was denied,—was it refuted?——The Secret Committee was appointed to enquire into the cause of the invasion of the Carnatic; but when the Lord Advocate first came forward in the House of Commons, the major part of his resolutions were pointed against Mr. Hastings, for acts done many years ago, most of them approved, some condemned, but himself acquitted by his constituents from every suspicion of being actuated by a corrupt motive, in any one transaction of his government. The two Committees cordially co-operated with each other; the grand object with each appeared to be the removal of Mr Hastings. The Secret committee, in an early stage of their enquiry, had discovered *the absolute necessity of sending Parliamentary Supervisors to India*;—the Select Committee, that three of their own body, General Smith, Mr. Rouse, and Mr. Dudley

Dudley Long, were admirably calculated to ſucceed Mr. Haſtings, Mr. Macpherſon, and Mr. Stables. The Lord Advocate, after laying the reſolutions of the Secret Committee upon the table of the Houſe, moved for a day for voting or rejecting them; but Major Scott, the Agent of Mr. Haſtings, having humbly repreſented to him the impropriety of voting theſe reſolutions, before the reports on which they were ſuppoſed to be grounded had been printed, the Advocate was pleaſed to put off the conſideration of them for a fortnight. In the mean time, General Smith moved the recal of Sir Elijah Impey, and declared he ſhould have moved the recal of Mr. Haſtings alſo, had he not underſtood that a motion to that effect was to be made by the Lord Advocate from the Secret Committee. At laſt, Sir, the important moment arrived—the Lord Advocate was ill, and abſent;—after ſome private converſation between Mr. Burke, General Smith, and Sir Adam Ferguſon, the latter brought up the famous forty-four reſolutions of the Secret Committee: from the gallery I could count but twenty-ſix Members in the Houſe, moſt of them belonging to the two Committees: the reſolutions were read and voted, with this remarkable circumſtance, that the only word which could be ſuppoſed, even by a forced conſtruction, to convey a perſonal reflection upon Mr. Haſtings, was expunged. Sir Adam then propoſed, as a 45th reſolution, "that it was the duty of the Court of Directors, to recal thoſe perſons whoſe conduct had been cenſured." This was alſo carried, although Mr. Robinſon, Member for Canterbury, remarked, with peculiar emphaſis, *that the Houſe was rather empty, conſidering the importance of the reſolution they were about to come to.* It paſſed, however; and was carried on the following day to the Directors by General Smith and Sir Henry Fletcher. On that day there was a Court of Proprictors, who received the reſolution for Mr. Haſtings's recal with ſuch evident marks of ſurprize and diſcontent, that although it had paſſed in a Committee of the whole Houſe, it never was reported to the Honſe. On the 28th of May this reſolution, under a new form, was again brought forward by the Lord Advocate, who declared, when he propoſed it, that the abilities of Mr. Haſtings were of the moſt ſplendid kind, and his integrity undoubted. Mr. Fox made a ſimilar declaration. Mr. Powys, Mr. Huſſey, and, in ſhort, every Member who ſpoke on that remarkable day, Mr. Burke and General Smith excepted, acknowledged the abilities and the integrity of Mr. Haſtings, in the moſt expreſſive terms: but, upon the miſtaken idea that his ambition was boundleſs, it

was

was resolved, " that it was the duty of the Court of Directors to remove him." Mr. Burke was then in office, and he appeared bent upon procuring Mr. Hastings's removal, with a solicitude as earnest, and a vengeance as unrelenting, as he had so recently displayed in the persecution of the gallant Lord Rodney, on the evidence of two Jews, and a Swiss. All opposition was therefore vain; the friends of Mr. Hastings did not divide the House, which consisted of 43 Members; but Commodore Johnstone plainly told the Ministers of that day, if they were determined to remove Mr. Hastings, *that* was not the way to do it—the Directors would not obey a resolution of one branch of the legislature. Mr. Fox forgot himself so far on that occasion, from a desire to oblige his friend Mr. Burke, as to declare, that if the Directors should refuse to obey a resolution of the House of Commons, they ought to be impeached: yet did I hear this same Mr. Fox, *this consistent Statesman*, assert, a few days afterwards in the debate upon Mr. Rigby's balances, that all the world knew a resolution of the House of Commons was of no effect—that no man, or body of men, was bound to pay obedience to it! How shall we reconcile this declaration to Mr. Fox's proposed impeachment of the Directors?

The resolution thus passed, was sent to the Court of Directors; but they were prevented from proceeding upon it, by the interference of the Court of Proprietors, who have declared that they will give up their charter, rather than consent to the removal of Mr. Hastings until some ground of delinquency can be proved against him. An enquiry into his conduct has commenced at the India-House. Under this enquiry, his friends are perfectly easy; they wish to promote it to the utmost of their power, being fully convinced that an unprejudiced Court of Proprietors will find it to have been, what the Secret Committee of the House of Commons declared it was upon several very critical occasions, wise, spirited, prudent, just, and proper.

Mr. Fox, in his famous speech in the House of Commons, has said, that there were other causes of difference between Lord Shelburne and himself, " that Lord Shelburne wanted to screen some East-India culprits." If Lord Shelburne was averse to the removal of Mr. Hastings in the present most critical state of the Company's affairs, I avow, that he acted the part of a wise minister, and an honest man!

ASIATICUS.

For the MORNING HERALD.

LETTER IX.

Mr. Editor.

IN the letter which I addressed to you a few days ago, I concisely, and I hope impartially, related the steps taken by the two Committees of the House of Commons, to remove Mr. Hastings from the government of Bengal: I shall now trouble you with a few remarks on the conduct of the Gentlemen in Leadenhall-street, first however observing, that all men who are conversant in the affairs of the East-India Company, or interested in its prosperity, must recollect, that during the time the Secret Committee was sitting, it was repeatedly asserted, by many anonymous writers, "that Mr. Hastings "was the author of the Maratta war." Mr. Francis has said in his pamphlet, that Mr. Hastings's denial of this fact, would be received with universal astonishment. In reply to this assertion, Major Scott publicly avowed, that Mr. Hastings would be warranted in having made that declaration, by the reports of the Secret Committee. Those, with the appendix to each, make two very large volumes in folio; I mean those reports only which contain the rise and progress of the Maratta war; but as I fear, Mr. Editor, few men will search for truth amidst such a mass of matter, I shall rest the propriety of Major Scott's assertion, upon a declaration which fell from the Lord Advocate himself:—"that the Maratta war originated in "Bombay, and was encouraged and approved of by the Court "of Directors." The Lord Advocate was induced to make this confession, by Mr. Powys having declared it to be his opinion, "that Mr. Hastings was not the author of the Maratta "war." Although he was freed from this burthen, there were other parts of his conduct which induced the House to determine,

mine, " that it was the duty of the Court of Directors to re-" move him."

It was thought proper, on the 20th of June, to call a General Court of Proprietors, for the express purpose of taking this vote into consideration; so respectable a meeting had not appeared at the India House for many years: the subject was fairly and ably argued, notwithstanding the attempt of an illustrious lawyer to divert the attention of the Proprietors from the important object of their deliberation. The conclusion which the Court came to was decent, just, and proper:— " that to remove Mr. Hastings, merely in compliance with a " vote of one branch of the Legislature, without being first " convinced of his delinquency, would be to give up the in-" dependency of the Company." It was further resolved, " that no steps were to be taken respecting his removal, with-" out a previous communication to the Proprietors."

I speak with tenderness, and without resentment, of the respectable Gentleman who lately filled the Chair of the Direction; but surely, Sir, there was a strange absurdity in the conduct of this business from the first to the last. That Gentleman had been an active Member of the Secret Committee; he consented to, he supported the mode adopted for effecting Mr. Hastings's removal; but when he spoke behind the bar at the India House, he said, " To be sure a vote of one branch of the Legislature is not to influence the Directors;"—yet he was in the House of Commons, Sir Henry Fletcher was there, and I believe Mr. Wilkinson too, when Mr. Fox made that unconstitutional declaration, that if the Directors did not conform to the vote of the House, they ought to be impeached.

I think, Sir, if I had had the honor of sitting in Parliament, of being a Member of the Secret Committee, and a Director of the East-India Company, and had been conscientiously of opinion, that Mr. Hastings ought to be removed, I would have resorted to the true constitutional mode of effecting it; I would have assisted in *bringing in a bill* for his removal; but I never could have joined in voting that it was my duty, and the duty of my brother Directors, to remove him for acts, on which we had already passed either censure or approbation. A moment's reflection will convince any reasonable man upon what different principles an enquiry at the India House, and in Parliament, must be carried on: the latter may commence their enquiry at any period they think proper; but can the former, with propriety, do so? The limits of this letter will not allow me to enter so fully into this subject as I could wish; but I will endeavour to explain myself in a few words: the Secret

Committée censure Mr. Hastings for with-holding the King's tribute, and for his concern in the Rohilla war: For the last transaction, Mr. Powys was of opinion Mr. Hastings should be recalled. It was, however, commenced and ended in six months of the year 1774, and the Proprietors pronounced judgment upon it in 1775. The stoppage of the King's tribute, under all the circumstances which attended it, was highly approved of: yet the House of Commons state these acts, amongst others, as grounds for resolving, "that it is the duty of the "Court of Directors to remove Mr. Hastings." If any new lights can be thrown upon the former transactions in Bengal, it is undoubtedly the duty of the Court of Directors to reconsider them, otherwise their decision has already gone forth, or they have been grossly negligent of their duty. They constantly receive advices from Bengal, and of course answer the letters they receive: the Directors can therefore finish their enquiry very shortly, since they have only to consider those advices which have arrived subsequent to the close of their last dispatches. Had they thought Mr. Hastings unworthy to remain in their service, they might have removed him by an address to the Crown, nor would he have been favoured by his Majesty's late Ministers. But so far was his conduct from subjecting him to such a disgrace, that in looking over such of the Company's general letters as are printed in the sixth report of the Secret Committee, I find great commendations bestowed upon him, for his negociations with the Nizam, and for the manly, decided, and spirited exertions, by which he preserved the Carnatic.

I cannot conclude this letter without observing, that integrity and abilities may be serviceable to a man, even in these degenerate days. Mr. Hastings, an unconnected individual, without borough influence, or an overgrown fortune, but merely by the weight of his personal character, hath been able to defeat the attempts of one branch of the Legislature, and of a popular Administration to remove him from his government. Let it be remembered, that Mr. Burke and Mr. Fox strained every nerve to carry this point when they were Ministers of this country; when they possessed a great share of popularity, the former by his reputation for disinterestedness, and the latter acquired by his positive and unequivocal declaration that he could make peace with America, and would *ingage* to do it, even though Lord North was the Minister, provided the negociation was committed to him. If others of his Majesty's ministers were inclined to think more favourably of Mr. Hastings, as Mr. Fox has insinuated, they certainly sacrificed their inclinations to preserve

preſerve unanimity in the national councils, for Mr. Haſtings was preſerved by the virtuous efforts of a great majority of his moſt reſpectable conſtituents, by men *who could have no private views to gratify*, who had never been in habits of intimacy with him, and to moſt of them, he was not even perſonally known. To their everlaſting honor let it be obſerved, that they would not conſent to give up a man, who had faithfully and ſucceſsfully ſerved them two-and-thirty years, becauſe Mr. Burke, in the hour of his greatneſs, had determined it ſhould be ſo. Of that gentleman's knowledge in India politics, they had ſome experience. He obtained a qualification in 1781, and attended upon party queſtions for a month or two. We can all of us recollect; how he confounded the Kriſtna, the Coleroon, and the Ganges, and what groſs ignorance he betrayed of the common rules of the ſervice. The knowledge which he has ſince acquired, has enabled him to diſcover, that, to ſave the Company, we muſt diſmiſs the ableſt Britiſh ſubject in India from our ſervice.

Much hath been ſaid, and great uſe was artfully made, of the firſt imperfect accounts which were received of the late revolution at Benares; a compleat narrative of that affair, written by Mr. Haſtings himſelf, has lately been received at the India-houſe. I truſt, that narrative will be laid before the Proprietors, and to the judgment of his conſtituents, and the public at large, Mr. Haſtings contentedly, and with pleaſure, ſubmits his conduct throughout that critical tranſaction.

Auguſt 13, 1782. ASIATICUS.

For

For the MORNING HERALD.

Mr. EDITOR,

A WRITER who calls himself *Asiaticus* seems a violent panegyrist of the present Governors of Bengal; he probably finds it convenient to be so; if he confined himself to his idol, his worship should be never disturbed by me, but when he reflects on others, who to my certain knowledge are as far superior to that fortunate monarch of Bengal as a learned parson is to an illiterate parish-clerk: I can't forbear animadverting on it.

Mr. Hastings, like many others employed in that great *Monopoly*, was luckily in the way to preferment when fortune presented two Ministers, who by dint of sound and solid reasons have procured him the strongest patronage he could wish, whereby, and by means of the distracted state of this unfortunate country, he has ruled the roast near twelve years in Bengal; his fortune, so far from not being overgrown, is known (though perhaps not to this essayist) to be immense; as to his negociation, refer to his concessions to the King of Cultac, his appointment of a crack-brain'd European (moorishly mad) to the command of Bengal reinforcement sent to the Carnatic after the brave Bailey's defeat, which took ten months to march one thousand miles; and to his last affair with Cheyk Sing at Benares, the most bungling affair that ever was concerted. In India, the Black Hole, and Patna massacres sink to nothing when compared with it, and let Mr. H. and his abettors do their utmost to conceal that, and the dreadful famine at Madrass, occasioned by Salt Agencies, and other selfish unfeeling motives: there are those, who disdaining falshood and flattery, will give the truth to the public, which sure no honest man, or friend to his country, can take amiss.

If you think proper to publish this, you may hear more from

August 17, 1782. A CONSTANT READER.

LETTER

For the MORNING HERALD.

LETTER X.

Mr. EDITOR,

IN Reply to a Letter signed *A Constant Reader*, I beg leave to observe, that as the writer has not attempted to controvert a single fact contained in my former Letters, a very few words from me will suffice.

I do not know, Mr. Editor, that I have reflected upon a single individual. It is true, indeed, I have been under the necessity of mentioning the names of Mr. Fox, Mr. Gregory, Mr. Burke, General Smith, Sir Henry Fletcher, and the lately elected Director, Mr. Wilkinson. Does he mean that these Gentlemen, or any of them, are superior characters to Mr. Hastings? It is well known they endeavoured to the utmost of their power to remove him from the Government of Bengal; but can he tell me, why they did not pursue the only constitutional mode of effecting it, after Commodore Johnstone had candidly assured them, that the resolution which *they had forced through a very thin House* would be opposed in Leadenhall-street? I beg leave to ask this writer what patronage has been procured for Mr. Hastings, or by whom? Was he not supported by his constituents the Indpendent Proprietors of East-India stock? Could this support have been purchased by money? The writer says, Mr. Hastings's fortune is known to be immense, yet adds in the same line, that he knows nothing of the matter. The severest enemies of Mr. Hastings in Parliament, and at the India-house, have borne ample testimony to his integrity and abilities. Here, then, I shall rest this point until some proof shall be produced, that his fortune is enormous. I shall barely observe in reply to the facts which are stated, that Colonel Pearse was six months, not ten, in marching to Madras; that he would have been there in four, if he had not halted by orders from Sir Eyre Coote; that so far from Mr. Hastings causing

causing a famine at Madras, Lord Macartney, and his Council, acknowledge in the warmest terms in their letter to the Court of Directors, that they had received the most effectual assistance and support from Bengal; that they had been amply supplied with men, money, and provisions, by the Supreme Council. The narrative of the late transactions at Benares is at the India-house; it is, or ought to be open for the inspection of the Proprietors, who will form their own judgment upon it.

August 19, 1782. ASIATICUS.

www.ingramcontent.com/pod-product-compliance
Lightning Source LLC
Chambersburg PA
CBHW031454270326
41930CB00007B/993

* 9 7 8 3 7 4 4 7 1 5 6 8 3 *